Your Window Greenhouse

Your Window

Drawings by Adrían Martínez

Greenhouse

John Bracken

THOMAS Y. CROWELL COMPANY
New York / Established 1834

Copyright © 1977 by JOHN BRACKEN
All rights reserved. Except for use in a review, the reproduction or utilization of this work in any form or by any electronic, mechanical, or other means, now known or hereafter invented, including xerography, photocopying, and recording, and in any information storage and retrieval system is forbidden without the written permission of the publisher. Published simultaneously in Canada by Fitzhenry & Whiteside Limited, Toronto.
Manufactured in the United States of America

Library of Congress Cataloging in Publication Data

Bracken, John, 1927-
    Your window greenhouse.

    Includes index.
    1. Greenhouses, window. 2. Greenhouse gardening. 3. Window gardening. I. Title.
SB416.3.K7 1977   635'.04'4   76-27884

ISBN 0-690-01193-8
ISBN 0-690-01199-7(pbk.)

10 9 8 7 6 5 4 3 2 1

Contents

INTRODUCTION: IT'S A GREEN WORLD!   1

1   **What Have You Got?**   3

   WINDOW GREENHOUSES: HOW MUCH?   5

   ADVANTAGES OF A WINDOW GREENHOUSE   7

2   **Planning the Window Greenhouse**   10

   PRACTICAL CONSIDERATIONS   11

   WHERE TO PUT THE WINDOW GREENHOUSE   13

   WHAT YOU CAN GROW   15

   GROWING CONDITIONS   17

   BEGINNER'S LIST OF PLANTS   18

3 Constructing the Window Greenhouse   20

ATTACHING THE GREENHOUSE TO THE WINDOW   21
- LEDGER STRIPS   21
- FLASHING   21
- BRACING   21

VENTILATION   23

SNOW PROTECTION   23

TOOLS   23
- HAMMER   24
- SCREWDRIVERS   24
- SAWS   24

MATERIALS   25
- LUMBER   25
- ALUMINUM   28
- GLASS, ACRYLIC, AND OTHER PLASTICS   28
- SALVAGE GLASS AND SASH   31

INJECTION-MOLDED WINDOW GREENHOUSES   31

INTERIOR WINDOW GREENHOUSES   33

SHELVES AND SUPPORTS   34

HEATING   37

PLANTERS   38

CONTAINERS   39

KINDS OF WINDOWS   40

GALLERY OF WINDOW GREENHOUSES   40

4 Growing Conditions in the Window Greenhouse   53

LIGHT EXPOSURE   54
- PLANTS FOR EAST AND SOUTH WINDOWS   55
- PLANTS FOR WEST WINDOWS   56
- PLANTS FOR NORTH WINDOWS   56

WATERING   57

SOIL   58

FEEDING 60

    GENERAL FEEDING RULES 61

POTTING 61

5 Decorative Plants for the Window Greenhouse 63

MINIATURES 65

CACTI AND OTHER SUCCULENTS 65

GESNERIADS 67

    AFRICAN VIOLET VARIETIES (MINIATURE) 68

    OTHER GESNERIADS 68

BEGONIAS 69

ORCHIDS 70

BROMELIADS 73

FOLIAGE PLANTS 74

    PHILODENDRONS 75

    FERNS 76

    DRACAENAS 79

    DIEFFENBACHIAS 80

ANNUALS AND PERENNIALS 80

    ANNUALS 82

    PERENNIALS 85

OTHER PLANTS 86

6 Food Plants for the Window Greenhouse 90

VEGETABLES 90

    BEETS 92

    CARROTS 92

    CUCUMBERS 93

    EGGPLANT 93

    LETTUCE 94

    PEPPERS 94

    SPINACH 95

    TOMATOES 95

HERBS 96
- BASIL 96
- DILL 96
- MARJORAM 97
- PARSLEY 97
- ROSEMARY 97
- SAGE 98
- SAVORY 98
- TARRAGON 98
- THYME 98

7 Starting New Plants in the Window Greenhouse 99

SOWING SEED 99

TAKING CUTTINGS 102
- LEAF CUTTINGS 103

8 Insects and Diseases 104

APHIDS 105

MEALYBUGS 105

RED SPIDER MITES 105

SCALE 107

THRIPS 107

OLD-FASHIONED PEST REMEDIES 108
- ALCOHOL SWABS 108
- NICOTINE 108
- SOAP AND WATER 108
- WATER SPRAY 109
- GROUND PEPPER 109
- BEER 109
- BOILING WATER 109

CHEMICAL PREVENTATIVES 109
- HOW TO USE CHEMICALS 110

DISEASES 111
- FUNGICIDES 112

WINDOW GREENHOUSE SUPPLIERS 113

INDEX 115

Introduction: It's a Green World!

The view from your window need never be barren or gray. It can be green all year round. How? Install a window greenhouse. No matter what kind of window you have—double-hung, casement, floor-to-ceiling, or sliding—whether you live in an apartment or a house, there is a window greenhouse for you. This book shows you how to build it and what to grow.

Window greenhouse gardening makes you a better gardener since many plants growing together are easy to water and furnish their own humidity (plants transpire through their leaves). Further, a grouping of plants is always a more pleasing display than a few plants on a windowsill. It is a showcase to gladden the eye and cheer the soul on every day of the year.

If you really want beautiful plants indoors there is

INTRODUCTION: IT'S A GREEN WORLD!

no excuse not to have them. Any window will do, and just what kind of arrangement you select, whether simple or elaborate, depends on your individual situation. This book discusses a wide variety of window greenhouses to choose from, to allow you to have lovely plants indoors all year without undue expense or labor.

All the basic designs as well as information on tools and supplies needed to set up your window greenhouse are included in these pages, together with a comprehensive listing of the many plants you can grow. Here is real garden magic; all you need is a window, some plants, this book in hand—and, of course, a love of nature.

John Bracken

1
What Have You Got?

The windowsill has traditionally been the place for growing plants indoors. Although many people still maintain windowsill gardens, today the window greenhouse has become more desirable. Such an enclosed area provides excellent environmental conditions for growing a wide variety of plants, including many that cannot survive on a windowsill, to create a display of color and greenery that can be viewed from within and without.

Window design and construction have changed through the years. The double-hung window—with top and bottom sash and wide sill—is still around, but more and more different types of window are replacing it in new construction. Before you make or buy your window greenhouse, you must consider the type of window you

WHAT HAVE YOU GOT?

are working with. (This is discussed in chapter 3.) Once you learn about the different types of greenhouses, you will be able to take almost any window and transform it into the garden you want.

The prefabricated window greenhouse is most often made of metal and glass and comes with all parts ready for assembly. Some fit several sizes of window, others only a specific size—so check before buying. (Photo by Matthew Barr)

Window Greenhouses: How Much?

While the commercially sold window greenhouse has been available for some time, it is only in recent years that its value has been recognized. And now there are prefabricated units of modest cost; some kits sell for as low as $59. Others retail for close to $300. They are made of glass or plastic in wooden or metal frames. Generally, all the prefab models provide the same function: to create a controlled environment for plants—the same as in a standard greenhouse but on a smaller scale.

If a prefabricated unit does not appeal to you or is too costly, you can always make your own window greenhouse. There are distinct advantages here. You can make the unit to fit any specific window. It can be made of any material you choose and can be designed in any of several ways to enhance the beauty or match the architectural style of your home.

Generally, a window greenhouse is attached outside a window—but if you make your own you can also have a window greenhouse inside a room. This way you have a total display area that can be viewed from all parts of the room. The indoor window greenhouse is not, at this writing, available as a package, but included here are several drawings of interior enclosed gardens you can make.

This homemade unit has a plywood base and is made from redwood molding and $1/4$-inch-thick acrylic. The installation was done from the outside. (Photo by Jerry Bagger)

No matter what kind of greenhouse you select—prefabricated or homemade, for outside or inside the window—final selection depends on how much money you want to spend and how many plants you want to grow. I have found that an average size of 30×48 inches will accommodate more than thirty plants. A garden of this size is not too much to care for, and, if you make your own, the greenhouse can be built for about $100.

A homemade window greenhouse with shelves and metal bins inserted. Thin square moldings hold the shelves in place. The sliding window has been retained to regulate ventilation. (Photo by Jerry Bagger)

Advantages of a Window Greenhouse

A greenhouse at a window offers a great deal for little cost, time, and effort. Even a half dozen plants furnish beauty and can satisfy the desire to have something of the outdoors indoors. As such, window greenhouses certainly have their place in today's home.

A one-piece molded acrylic unit is shown here. Available from manufacturers, such models are attractive, durable, weatherproof, and lightweight. (Photo courtesy Rohm and Haas Co.)

Window greenhouse gardening is more costly than windowsill gardening, but it offers so much more. Here you can grow almost everything you might want and are not restricted to certain plants that can tolerate a bit of abuse. You also can start seed and cuttings easily to save on plant costs. Of course in a controlled situation such as a window greenhouse you will want to grow many plants and thus will have to give more time to the garden. But it is time well spent because the results are so rewarding.

This special homemade window/door greenhouse extends beyond the wall at ground level. Its size permits cultivation of a great many plants. The outside structure is made of clear acrylic. (Photo by Jerry Bagger)

2 Planning the Window Greenhouse

When you add a window greenhouse to your home, you capture the outdoors indoors. You do not have to worry about whether there are trees and shrubs outside or gray concrete surrounding you. You can provide your own natural scene. And in this space you can grow plants all year because of the simulated conditions maintained there.

What you can grow depends on space; there is no other limitation. You can grow orchids, bromeliads, vegetables, herbs, even a few annuals and perennials. The kinds of plants feasible are not a problem—but space will be, so when planning the greenhouse take this factor into consideration; or install two window greenhouses.

As previously mentioned, you may want to build

The author's window greenhouse, in his office, provides a veritable jungle atmosphere; it is filled with houseplants of all kinds. (Photo by Jerry Bagger)

(or have built) your own window greenhouse, or you may want to buy a prefabricated one. Building a greenhouse is not difficult, as you will see from the several working drawings of different types of window greenhouse in this book. These greenhouses accommodate almost any type or size of window opening.

Practical Considerations

If you own your home, there is no problem as to whether the greenhouse may be attached to a window. However, in a rented apartment you should—and usually have to—secure permission from the owner; here a greenhouse that can be disassembled (and most window greenhouses can be) is the best answer. Usually a landlord will not object to the greenhouse because it adds to the property's appearance. And today even the most hardened superintendents have their own collections of greenery, so they are receptive to the idea of tenants having gardens.

If you build your own unit (or have it built), consider the materials available. Is metal better than wood, or is wood the answer? To many people wood is the ideal choice because it is natural looking and imparts a unified impression that never clashes with a building. On the other hand, metal has its pluses: it is rustproof and sleek in appearance. Note though that metal is harder to work with than wood.

Wood and glass have been used for this attractive greenhouse. The top has movable vents; the shelves are of redwood slats spaced an inch apart. Begonias, orchids, and bromeliads grow lavishly in this controlled environment. (Photo by Matthew Barr)

You can buy metal channels at supply yards, and wood molding at lumber dealers. The best wood for your greenhouse is redwood because it resists weathering; the best metal is aluminum because it resists rust. The wooden window greenhouse is less expensive to make than the metal unit by about 25 percent. The average wooden greenhouse for a 24 × 30-inch opening should not cost more than $100, and will probably cost less. Homemade metal units run about $125.

Should you buy a ready-made unit and assemble it, or make your own? I have already stated my preference, but if you do not have the time to make your own greenhouse or are not handy with tools, get a prefabricated unit. Prefab units come knocked down with all pieces included, and you put them together by following the accompanying instruction sheets. If you buy a prefab greenhouse ask if it can be installed from the inside, and always first determine whether you must remove the window frame or if you can leave it in place. With most prefab models the window frame can stay in place, but some units are so designed that it must be removed.

Where to Put the Window Greenhouse

When I decided I wanted a window greenhouse, it was hard to determine where it would have the maximum value because there were so many likely places. You too may be undecided as to where the greenhouse should be located in your home, so let's look at some of the possibilities.

Perhaps the most logical place is the kitchen—because people spend a good deal of time there, and a lovely green scene boosts the spirits early in the morning. And of course watering plants in the kitchen is convenient. The disadvantage in placing the greenhouse in the kitchen is that most kitchens have only one window; fresh air would be blocked when the window greenhouse was in place. If this is not objectionable, then the kitchen is the first choice.

The second best location for a window greenhouse is the bathroom; plants look good in bathrooms, soften-

A handsome homemade window greenhouse in a kitchen, housing African violets. This unit is not totally enclosed but rather opens to the kitchen. (Photo by Max Eckert, courtesy Paul DuPont Interior Design)

ing the sometimes harsh lines or sterile colors. And again, water is only an arm's length away.

A living or dining room does not work well with a greenhouse unless the unit is custom designed to look like part of the building rather than a tacked-on afterthought. But if the greenhouse is designed to coordinate with the rest of the architecture, it can be very handsome. Just remember to create a marriage of indoors and outdoors by putting some potted plants on the floor or at the sides of the window to create balance and proportion.

Cellars or basements should not be ignored either because these areas are fine places for greeneries. This was where my first window greenhouse ultimately took shape; it added beauty to the sterile basement and was a perfect retreat, a hidden place to work with plants.

The easiest installation of any window greenhouse is at ground level because, if necessary, you can work on the outside without ladders. If you live in a high-rise apartment building the unit must be assembled from the inside, which is possible with most (but not all) greenhouse models.

What You Can Grow

Undoubtedly you will be growing such houseplants as philodendrons and dieffenbachias. But do add some other beautiful plants, such as orchids, which will do splendidly in the window greenhouse. Begonias will

Orchids grow with hydrangeas in this window greenhouse. Note the circular opening at the top for additional ventilation. (Photo by Jerry Bagger)

thrive, especially the angel-wings, with their bright pink-and-white flowers. The smaller gesneriads, such as African violets and episcias, are excellent choices for the greenhouse, and a number of other flowering plants like streptocarpus and schizocentron are ideal. The thousands of miniature varieties are also perfect candidates for greenhouse cultivation.

You can also grow vegetables like eggplant, tomatoes, cucumbers, and peppers. Almost any midget vegetable variety will work well (forget vining squash, peas, and beans). Many herbs make excellent greenhouse subjects too.

You can even grow mosses and carnivorous plants—projects that are impossible under standard home conditions. However, you may not want to grow trailing plants in the window greenhouse; they take a great deal of space. And large decorator plants belong in the living room or dining room, not in the window, so forget that citrus or ficus tree.

Considering all you *can* grow, these exceptions are hardly a loss. Indeed, when you open a window to a greenhouse, you open a door to a new world of gardening.

Growing Conditions

Just what will the conditions be inside your window greenhouse? If the unit is built and installed properly, conditions will be similar to those in a regular greenhouse. That is, the temperature will be between 70° and 75°F by day and 10 or 15 degrees less at night, and the humidity will be between 30 and 60 percent—ideal conditions for hundreds of plants.

Hopefully the greenhouse will be in a south, east, or west window, where there is ample light. But if other buildings interfere with the sunlight or the greenhouse must occupy a north window, have no fear because there are numerous plants that can grow in shady places.

With a reasonable amount of light, favorable temperatures, sufficient humidity (the bugaboo of most houseplants), and correct watering, you will be able to have fresh and cheerful greenery and bloom all year long.

PLANNING THE WINDOW GREENHOUSE

Beginner's List of Plants

(See chapters 5 and 6 for plant descriptions.)

South or East Window

VEGETABLES:	Carrots
	Cucumbers (midget varieties)
	Green peppers (midget varieties)
	Japanese eggplant
	Radishes
	Tomatoes (midget varieties)
HERBS:	Marjoram
	Rosemary
	Tarragon
	Thyme
FLOWERING PLANTS:	Aphelandra
	Cacti and other succulents
	Crassula argentea
	Crossandra
	Dipladenia
	Lobivia
	Lycaste aromatica
	Parodia
	Thunbergia
	Zygocactus
FOLIAGE PLANTS:	Any type

West Window

VEGETABLES:	Lettuce
	Spinach
	Tomatoes

West Window (cont.)

FLOWERING PLANTS:
- Begonias (angel-wing)
- Bromeliads (guzmania)
- *Cologyne cristata*
- Columnea
- *Dendrobium pierardii*
- *Hoya carnosa*
- Kohleria
- *Oncidium ampliatum*
- *Rechsteinaria cardinalis*
- *Ruellia macrantha*

FOLIAGE PLANTS: Any type

North Window

FLOWERING PLANTS:
- Anthurium
- Begonias (rex)
- Bromeliads (neoregelia, nidularium, vriesia)
- Campanula
- Gloxinia
- *Lantana montevidensis*
- Saintpaulia (African violets)

FOLIAGE PLANTS:
- Dieffenbachia
- Dracaena
- Philodendron

Caladiums flourish in this upper-story greenhouse. Note the bracing at the bottom.
(Photo by Jerry Bagger)

3 Constructing the Window Greenhouse

Don't let the idea of building your own window greenhouse frighten you, because almost anyone can nail and saw and insert glass or plastic. The main problem in greenhouse construction is attaching the unit to the window; some expertise is needed here because you must have a perfect seal. But by following the working drawings and plans in this book you should be able to both assemble and install your own unit properly. (Greenhouses for almost all types of window are included.)

Attaching the Greenhouse to the Window

It is most important that the seal be free of leaks, cracks, or openings of any kind. You want the greenhouse to fit flush into the window, like a letter in an envelope. Sealing tapes and compounds are available if you should find after construction that there are some leaks.

Ledger Strips

To attach the greenhouse properly you will need top, bottom, and side ledger strips. These strips are generally of 1×3-inch lumber; they form the greenhouse frame. The greenhouse slots into the frame and is secured with screws or nails.

Flashing

To secure a perfect seal between the house wall and greenhouse, some type of flashing—usually sheet metal or galvanized metal—should be used. Apply the material under the ledger strips.

Bracing

Bracing is not needed usually for small units, but for any unit over 24×36 inches screw or toenail in 2×4-inch braces at a 45-degree angle.

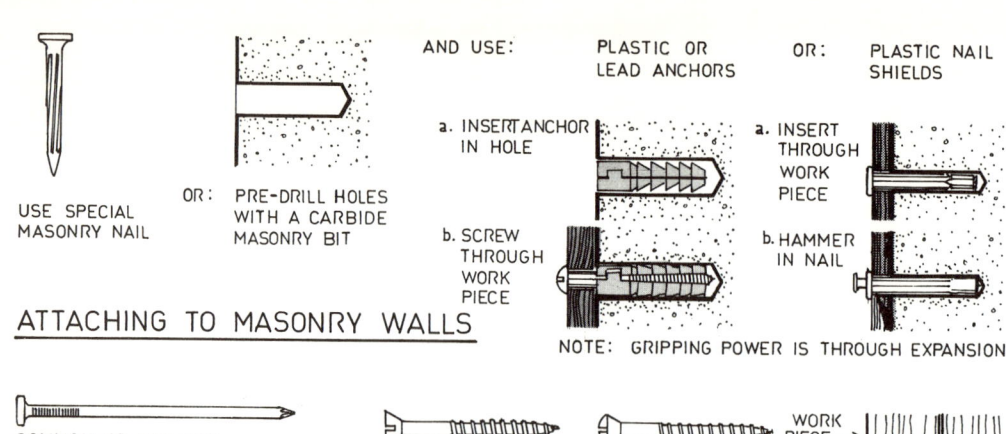

ATTACHING TO MASONRY WALLS

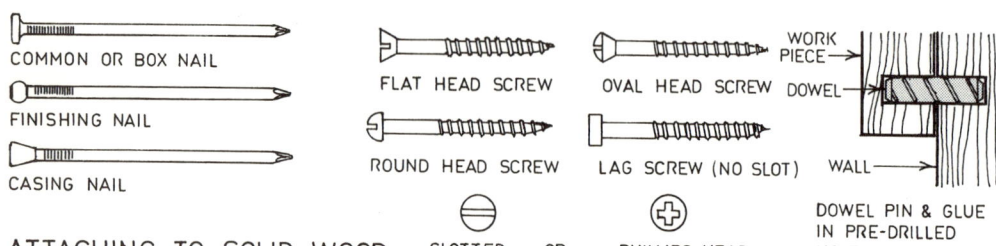

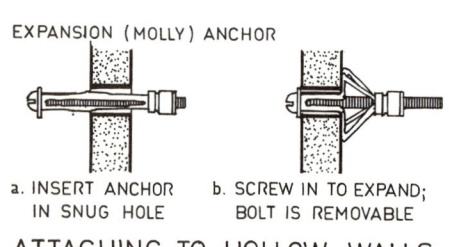

ATTACHING TO SOLID WOOD

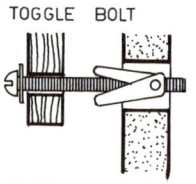

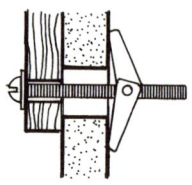

ATTACHING TO HOLLOW WALLS

FLASHING:
GALVANIZED METAL, ALUMINUM OR PLASTIC NAILED OR SCREWED TO WALL WITH A SEALER IN BETWEEN

SEALING AT WALLS

WEATHERSTRIPPING
a. METAL AND FELT
b. ADHESIVE PLASTIC FOAM
c. RUBBER GASKET
d. CAULKING CORD
e. SPRING BRONZE

SEALERS
a. CAULK
b. ASPHALT
c. PUTTY
d. SILICONE
e. ROOFING COMPOUND

NOTE: FOLLOW MANUFACTURER'S DIRECTIONS FOR APPLICATION

Attaching & Sealing

Ventilation

If you do not make a hinged top for your greenhouse so you can regulate ventilation within, drill a 4-inch hole in each side of the greenhouse so air can circulate. Fit the holes with hardware cloth in summer; fill them with wooden stoppers in winter if necessary.

Snow Protection

In some climates the weight of snow might be damaging to the greenhouse roof. A pitched roof helps but still may not alleviate problems with very heavy snow, so if you live in a severe winter climate be sure this portion of the window greenhouse is well constructed so it can hold additional weight if necessary.

Tools

The basic hand tools needed for building your window greenhouse are the same ones you probably have on hand for home carpentry work: hammer, screwdrivers, drills, pliers, plane, saws. You do not need any other tools for your construction.

Hammer

A claw hammer is the tool most used in wood construction, for driving in and pulling out nails. Try to get a drop-forged steel hammer heavy enough to feel comfortable in your hand. For metalwork you need a ball-peen hammer. Always buy the best possible hammer you can afford; a cheap one can ruin the material.

Screwdrivers

For either homemade or prefab greenhouse installation you will need several good screwdrivers. Buy two or three matched to various screw sizes. Start screw holes with a drill before inserting screws; this is much easier than screwing directly into the wood or metal.

Saws and Other Tools

Electric saws are convenient to use. However, if you are buying a saw, a standard handsaw (rip or crosscut) is sufficient for wood construction, a hacksaw for a prefab unit.

You may also need some pliers for work on a metal greenhouse, or a plane for wood construction. Some glass cutters will also come in handy for cutting glass to specific sizes if necessary.

Materials

Lumber

Use redwood or kiln-dried cedar heartwood for greenhouse frames because these are the only woods that resist moisture, decay, and insects. If you use woods like Douglas fir or pine, you must protect them from moisture with a sealing agent (sold at paint stores).

The amount of lumber required for your window greenhouse depends on the size of the structure, but basically you need 2×4-inch corner posts, rabbeted to accept the appropriate thickness of glass or acrylic, and side and base rails. (What you are doing is building a frame for the glass or acrylic.) Or you can use instead prerabbeted picture molding, which has indentations to hold glass or acrylic.

For a glass greenhouse, make the basic frame first and then install the glass. Slant the top of the greenhouse so rain will run off, and attach an exterior-grade plywood base. With an acrylic unit, first cement the sides and front; use ½-inch exterior-grade plywood for a base. Attach this rectangular box to the window, then add the top.

To attach either unit to the window, place 2×6-inch boards flat against the house wall on all four sides and bolt the boards in place. These are the anchor boards for the greenhouse frame. Small openings can be caulked with glazing compound.

This close-up photo shows the general construction of a redwood unit. Note the rabbeted moldings for the glass. (Photo by Matthew Barr)

A plywood base is used for this acrylic window unit (shown lying lengthwise). The acrylic is first predrilled—note the holes at the extreme edges. (Photo by Matthew Barr)

The sides and top of the acrylic greenhouse have been epoxied; tape helps to bind the seal. (Photo by Matthew Barr)

Anchor boards being installed on the outside of the house to accept the acrylic window greenhouse. (Photo by Matthew Barr)

Aluminum

Aluminum is used mainly for prefab window greenhouse frames because it is relatively inexpensive, lightweight, and sturdy. Also, it does not warp or rot and does not require a protective coat of paint. But aluminum has two major drawbacks: it looks sterile, and it is somewhat more difficult to work with than wood—cutting is more tedious.

Glass, Acrylic, and Other Plastics

For permanent installation, the greenhouse cover should be glass or acrylic. For a temporary cover, flexible plastic is all right. If you live in a cold climate, you may want to double-glaze the panes of the greenhouse; leave a ½-inch air space between the two pieces of glass or acrylic to cut heat loss approximately 30 percent.

Glass is sold on the even inch at glass shops; have the people at the shop cut the glass to size for you. Wear gloves when handling glass to prevent cuts. Ask for double strength glass of B quality (DSB). This glass, approximately ⅛ inch thick, is fine for most greenhouses. If you want thicker panes ask for $7/32$-inch crystal—but remember that the thicker the glass, the heavier the piece. Glaze the glass in wooden sashes with caulking compound (sold at glass stores).

Acrylic is also sold in even inches. If you use four

A prefabricated metal-and-glass greenhouse for a window. Ventilators are at the sides. Rubber molding assures a tight seal. (Photo by Matthew Barr)

sheets of acrylic for the greenhouse, as is most often done, you can have the sheets cut to size. Acrylic's great advantage is its relatively light weight. Select ¼-inch-thick acrylic, and install it as you would glass. Join the sheets at the cut edges with sealant (available at acrylic dealers). The bonding is simple to do, watertight, and permanent. Because window greenhouses are full of plants, obscuring a clear view of the panes themselves, you can economize by buying acrylic seconds. These have some hairline scratches but are much cheaper than first quality acrylic.

If you want a temporary cover for the window greenhouse—perhaps you do not have enough money at

CONSTRUCTING THE WINDOW GREENHOUSE

the moment—use any of the flexible plastics that lumber yards carry. Flat rigid plastic can also be used, but you cannot see clearly through it and it is not handsome in the home.

Glass, acrylic, and other plastics have relative advantages and disadvantages. Be aware of these before you select a cover.

MATERIAL	DESCRIPTION	INSTALLATION	REMARKS
Window glass (DSB type)	$1/8$-inch thickness	Glazing compound, clips	Suitable for small units up to 24 × 36 inches
Tempered glass	$1/4$-inch thickness	Glazing compound, clips	Expensive but almost unbreakable
Crystal	$3/16$-inch or $7/32$-inch thickness	Glazing compound, clips	Slightly wavy but otherwise excellent; for units over 24 x 36 inches
Thermopane (double-glazed)	Two pieces of glass with air space between	Have glazed professionally	Expensive but holds heat in the greenhouse (worth the money)
Acrylic sheet	Solid plastic available in several thicknesses	Nailed, glued, or screwed in place	Lightweight, but may turn yellow in time
Flexible plastic	Almost clear	Stapling gun	Temporary
Fiberglass panels	Flat or corrugated sheets in colors	Nailed or screwed in place	Rattle in wind; eventually must be replaced
Plastic screen	Wire embedded in plastic	Stapling gun	Can last a year

Salvage Glass and Sash

Can you use salvage glass and sash for window greenhouses? Yes, if it is readily available and inexpensive—today some salvage items cost more than new ones! What you probably can find for little money is window sash and shower doors that have been pulled out of old buildings. If you are very handy with tools and want to use salvage materials, certainly give them a try—you will save some money though not much.

It is hard to find salvage window glass because most of it is broken up and recycled to smelting companies. However, if you have discarded windows at home, cut out the panes and use them for your greenhouse.

Injection-Molded Window Greenhouses

I have added this section on the molded plastic window greenhouse because several companies are now making them, and quite frankly for the price they offer a great deal. A standard small unit of about 24 x 36 inches costs $60. The one-piece injection-molded process means that there is no chance of air leakage, which can sometimes occur in metal-and-glass or wood-and-glass installations. The units generally (but not always) come with

For a few plants the one-piece bubble molded unit is very suitable. It ensures a tight fit against the house. The existing window remains in place. (Photo courtesy Feather Hill Industries Inc.)

The bubble unit seen from inside the room. (Photo courtesy Feather Hill Industries Inc.)

flange plates for attachment to the window. Various kinds of sealing tape can be used to further ensure a tight seal between the house and greenhouse.

Interior Window Greenhouses

At one time I ran into a situation in which there just was not room outside for the conventional window greenhouse, that is, one that extends *out* from the wall. I decided to build an inner enclosure, with doors, around the window; this window greenhouse would extend *into* the room. At first I was a bit uncertain. Would the greenhouse take up too much room space? Would it look bad? Theoretically, the answer was yes to both questions. But I went ahead with my idea anyway.

I built a bookcase-type shelf system of simple construction in front of the window, with wooden doors at the front and acrylic sheet at the sides. My first inside window greenhouse had been created at a cost of only $40, and the unit looked so great that it added to rather than detracted from the room. The green "island" provided a handsome display, and I could control its temperature and humidity by merely opening or closing the greenhouse doors.

What is the difference between an outside window greenhouse and an inside one like this? Primarily light—the outside unit receives more sunshine. (Of course installing fluorescent tubes in the interior greenhouse can improve matters.) But other than that, the principle is basically the same; both offer the house or apartment gardener an easy way to grow hundreds of plants.

Shelves and Supports

Most prefabricated window greenhouses come with glass shelves, but if you make your own greenhouse you must provide shelves and supports yourself. In my acrylic greenhouse I used acrylic bars, which I purchased cut to size from the supplier. I cemented these to the sides and inserted glass shelves. This is an easy installation and works very well. (Other supporting devices are shown in the drawings.)

The support that holds the shelf must be anchored securely to the window greenhouse itself to hold the shelf and the weight of your plants. Haphazard construction will cause accidents with falling plants, so do be careful and really secure the supports in place —whether they are wood, acrylic, or whatever.

While glass and acrylic are the accepted shelving materials, waffle-type plastics and preformed rigid plastic devices can also be used; wire shelving, too, is an alternative choice, but it is rarely esthetically pleasing. If installed properly, wood looks handsome; use redwood strips spaced ½ inch apart on suitable supports. This type of wooden shelving allows air to enter the bottoms of the pots, which is good for the plants; its disadvantage is that it blocks some light. Acrylic and glass of course allow maximum light to reach the plants.

A small prefabricated window greenhouse, painted white. Shelves are of hardware cloth. (Photo by Matthew Barr)

A wooden unit under construction has a waffle-type bottom that allows aeration. (Photo by Matthew Barr)

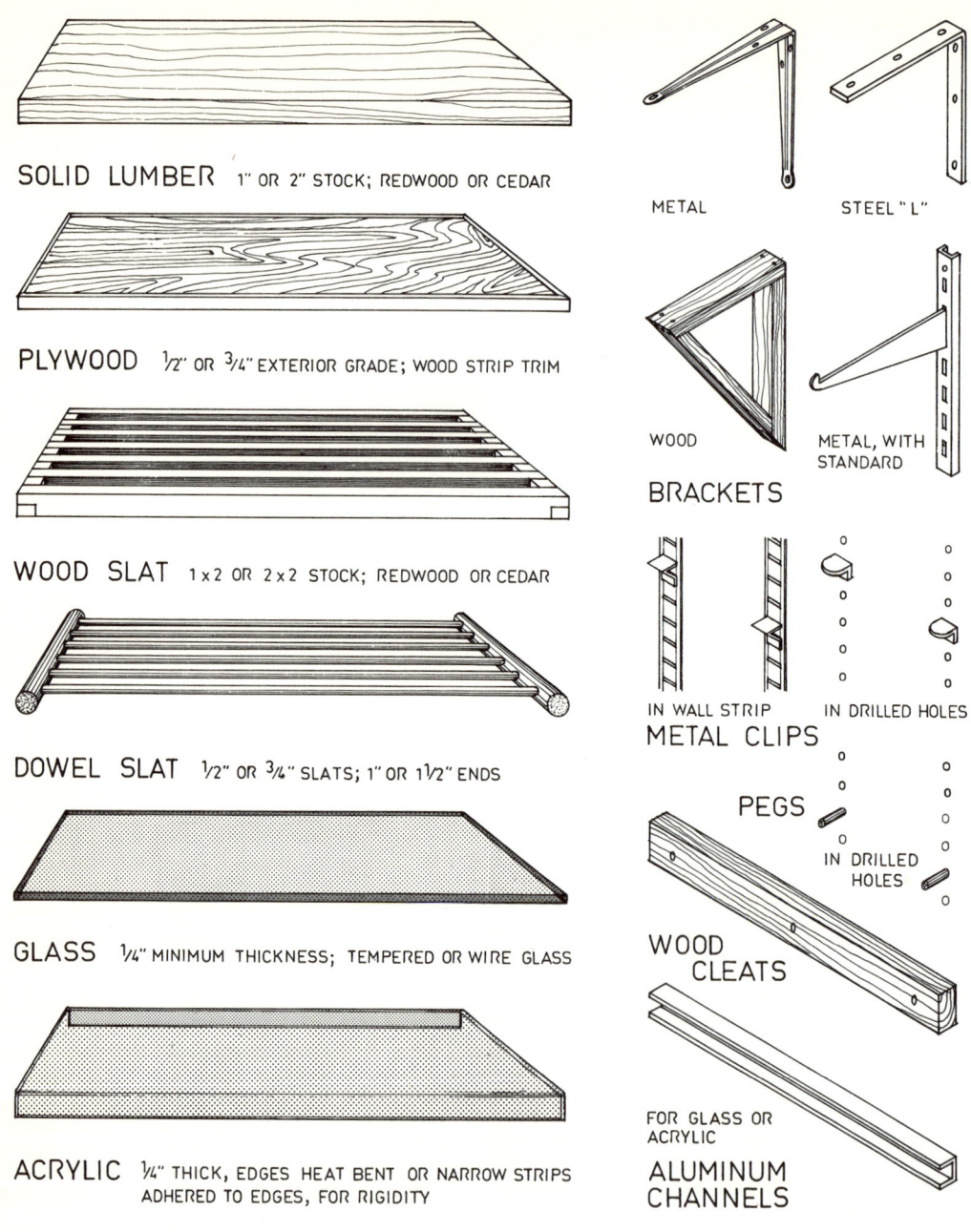

Shelves & Supports

In any case, no matter what the material, do not try to span more than 30 inches without installing midsupports—unless you are using acrylic or glass at least ¼ inch thick. Clay pots filled with soil can by very heavy! My window greenhouse is 40 inches in width, and I used ¼-inch crystal glass shelves; each holds twelve 8-inch pots satisfactorily.

Heating

If the window greenhouse is properly built and there are no air leaks, it should maintain a moderate temperature, even on cold nights. You can regulate temperature and air circulation by opening or closing the window. If you live in a region with very cold winters, you might want to install some weather-stripping; or insert a sheet of flexible plastic about 1 inch from the glass or acrylic to form an air cushion that keeps heat in the greenhouse. Another solution is to use a small space heater (the type used for heating bathrooms); these heaters are sold in department and drug stores. Keep a thermometer inside the greenhouse so you can tell the temperature at a glance. During winter nights try to maintain a minimum temperature of 60°F.

Ventilating the greenhouse is no problem if you have a hinged top and existing window sash to make adjustments. If it gets excessively hot or stuffy in the growing area, try a small fan at low speed.

CONSTRUCTING THE WINDOW GREENHOUSE

Planters

A planter is usually made of wood, but metal planter bins look neater in the window greenhouse. These are deep boxes made to fit specific areas within the greenhouse. The bin will look best if you can recess it so that the top is flush with the bottom of the windowsill.

Planter bins made of galvanized metal are available at sheet metal shops. The bins are welded together at the seams and have rolled edges so you cannot cut your hands. Have the supplier put in ¼-inch drain holes —about eight holes in an average 16 x 20-inch box. You can use shallower planters for annuals and perennials or for seed starting.

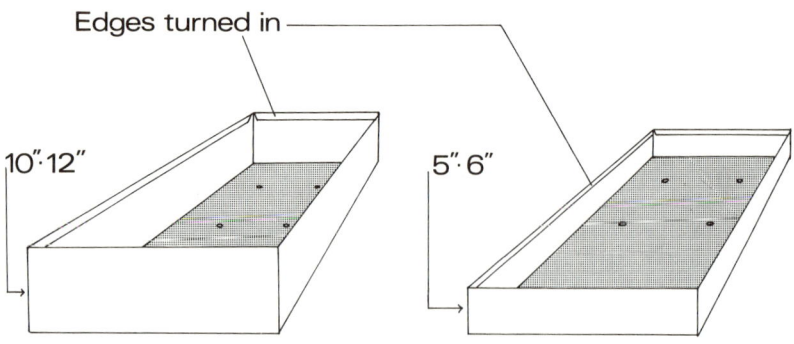

DEEP SHEET METAL   SHALLOW SHEET METAL

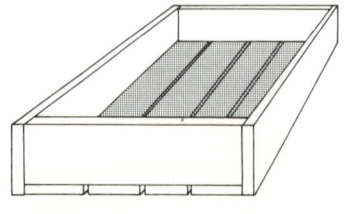   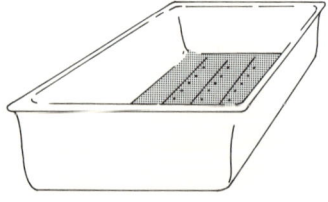

WOODEN FLAT   PLASTIC TRAY

Planter Boxes

Containers

In addition to planters, you will also want standard containers and decorative pots. Remember that the window greenhouse is open to the room and so becomes part of the interior. It should be esthetically pleasing—and this means that plants should be in handsome containers.

The choice of pots is vast: terra cotta containers are perhaps the most popular; plastic and clear acrylic pots are also attractive. There are also brass containers, baskets, cachepots, and so forth. Select containers of suitable colors and materials that harmonize with the room.

No matter what kind of containers you choose for your plants, it is wise to also buy the appropriate saucers for them. Excess water dripping over shelves is unsightly and in some cases may harm plants on another shelf—many plants resent moisture at the crown and may rot.

An acrylic greenhouse shown attached, with galvanized metal bins for plants. Note that they are flush with the sill. (Photo by Matthew Barr)

Kinds of Windows

The type of window you have will determine just how to approach the installation of the window greenhouse. In some cases, such as with a double-hung window, it is not necessary to remove the window itself. If you are in a building with casement windows that open out (or that open in, if you want an interior window greenhouse), then of course the window must be removed before the greenhouse can be attached. Generally, an awning-type window that opens in or out also requires removal.

If you are in a newer building that has sliding windows, the window need not be removed if installation is done from the outside. Indeed, the window itself acts as a door to the greenhouse that can be used to adjust ventilation and temperature.

Gallery of Window Greenhouses

The drawings on pages 43 through 52 show installation of greenhouses for many different window styles, providing you with information to guide you in almost any situation. Personal taste enters the picture too; some people like the existing window removed while others prefer to have it remain.

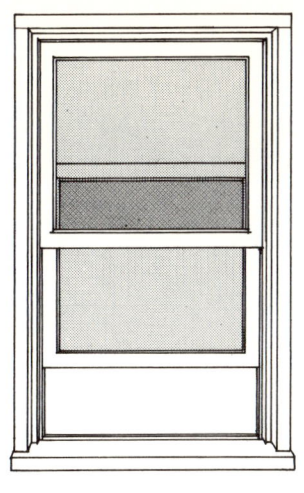

DOUBLE-HUNG
WOOD, ALUMINUM

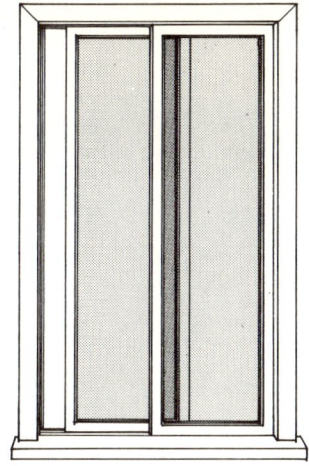

SLIDING
ALUMINUM, WOOD

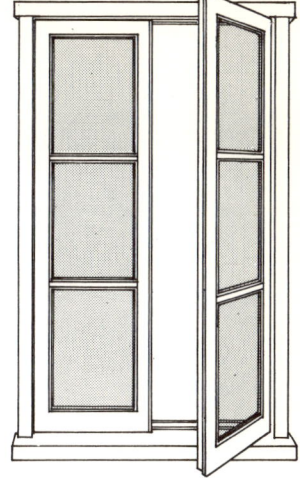

CASEMENT
WOOD, STEEL

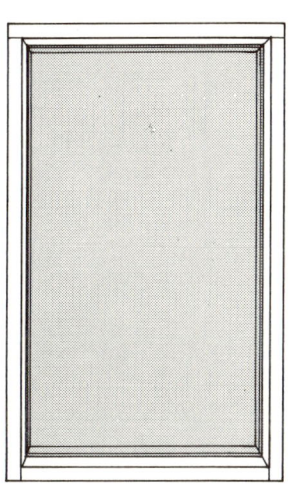

FIXED
WOOD, ALUMINUM, STEEL

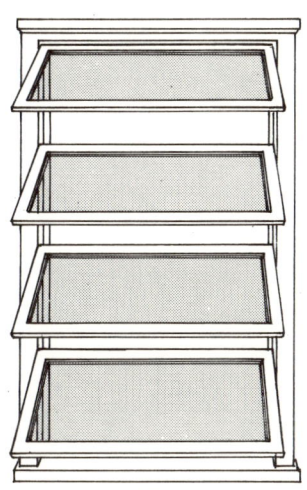

AWNING
ALUMINUM, STEEL

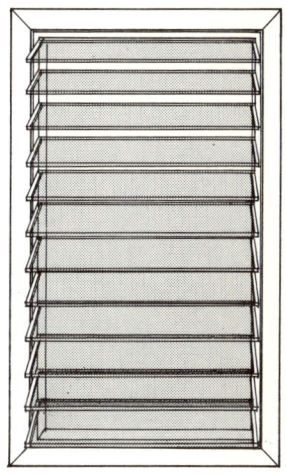

JALOUSIE
ALUMINUM

Standard Window Types

DOUBLE-HUNG WINDOW

1. STARTING AT THE BOTTOM WITH A CHISEL PRY OUT THE INSIDE STOP STRIP, PROGRESSIVELY MOVING ON TO EACH NAIL UNTIL THE STRIP CAN BE REMOVED ON ONE SIDE.
2. PULL THE SASH TOWARD YOU ON THAT SIDE AND OUT OF THE OPPOSITE GROOVE.
3. LIFT OUT THE SASH AND REMOVE THE SASH CORD FROM EACH SIDE.

NOTE: IF THERE IS T-STRIP WEATHERSTRIPPING IT MUST BE REMOVED ON THE SAME SIDE AS THE STOP BEFORE THE SASH CAN COME OUT.

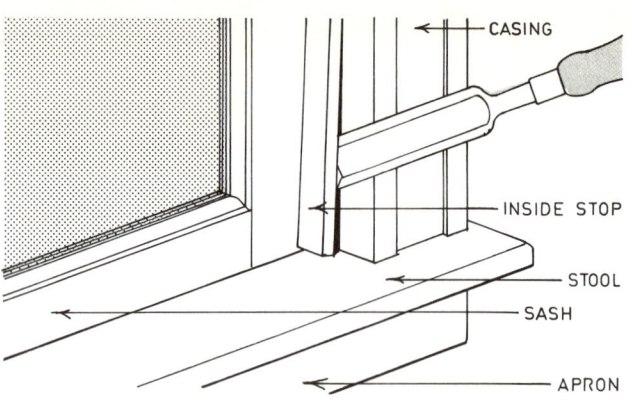

SLIDING WINDOW

1. UNSCREW THE RELEASE SCREWS ON EACH SIDE OF THE SLIDING SASH AND SLIP DOWN TO RETRACT THE INSIDE HEAD STOPS.
2. LIFT THE SASH UP AND OUT FROM THE BOTTOM TO REMOVE.
3. IF THERE IS A SCREEN, REMOVE BY LIFTING UP AND OUT FROM THE BOTTOM.
4. DEPENDING UPON THE CONSTRUCTION, REMOVE THE FIXED SASH BY UNSCREWING OR BY REMOVING THE CENTRE FRAME PIECE THEN LIFTING THE SASH UP AND OUT AT THE BOTTOM.

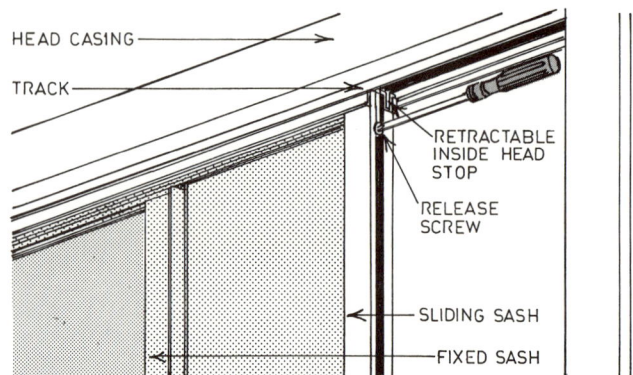

CASEMENT WINDOW

1. IF THERE IS AN OPERATOR ARM AND CRANK, REMOVE THE ARM BY DISENGAGING OR BY UNSCREWING.
2. REMOVE ALL HINGES BY UNSCREWING TO REMOVE SASH.

NOTE: IN THE CASE OF STEEL CASEMENT WINDOWS, REMOVE THE ENTIRE FRAME BY REMOVING THE INSIDE STOPS AS IN THE DIRECTIONS FOR THE DOUBLE-HUNG WINDOW ABOVE.

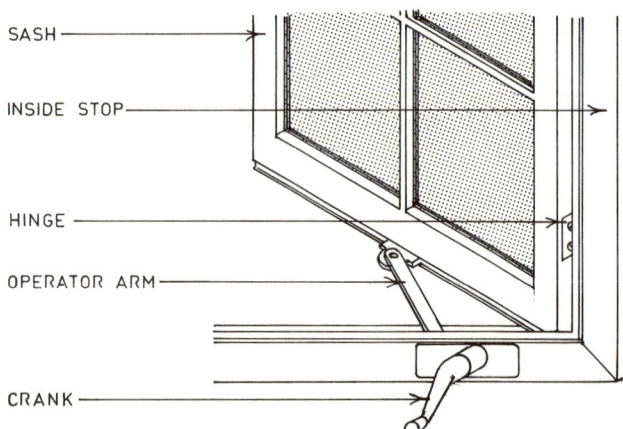

Window Removal

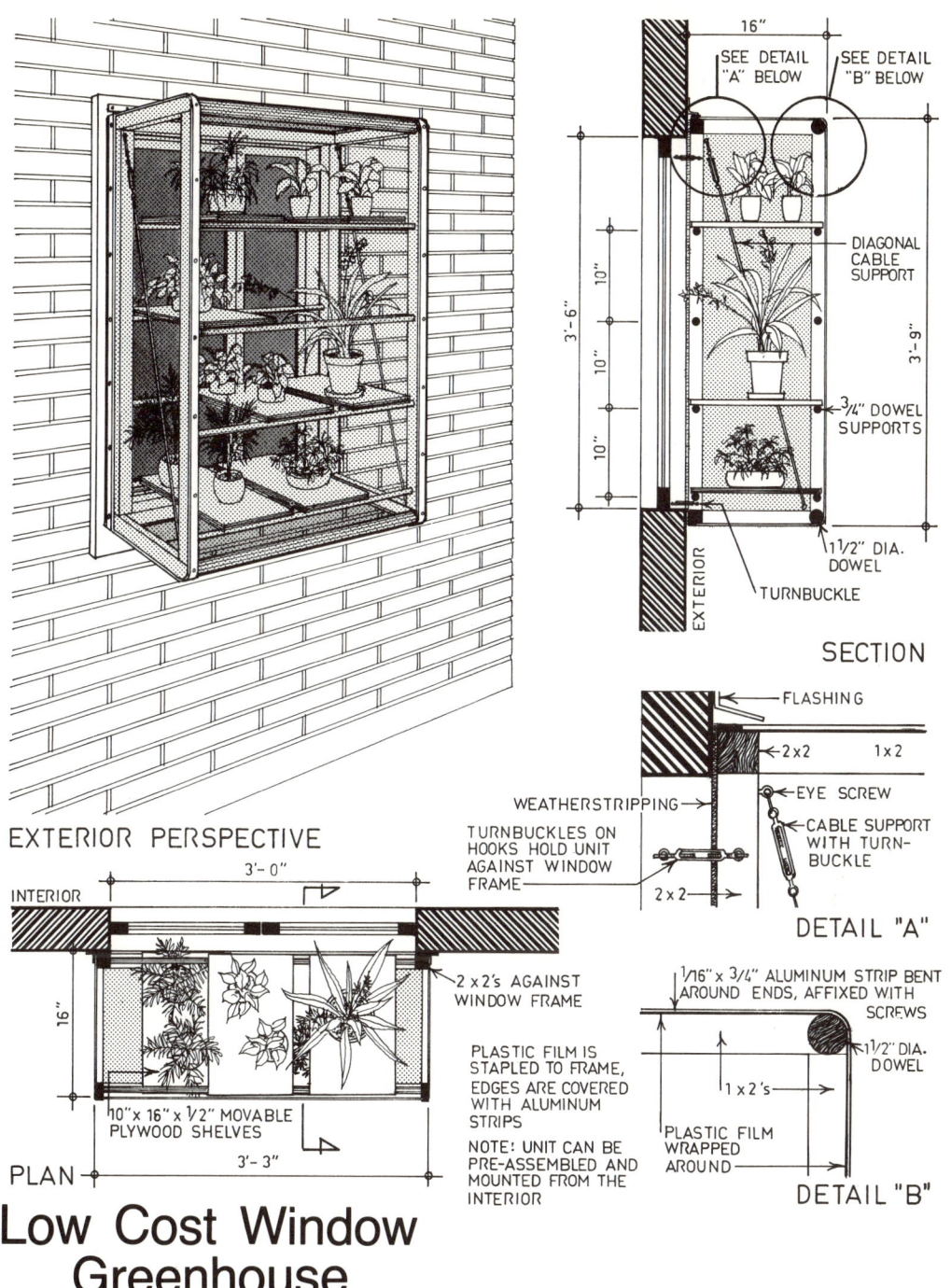

Low Cost Window Greenhouse

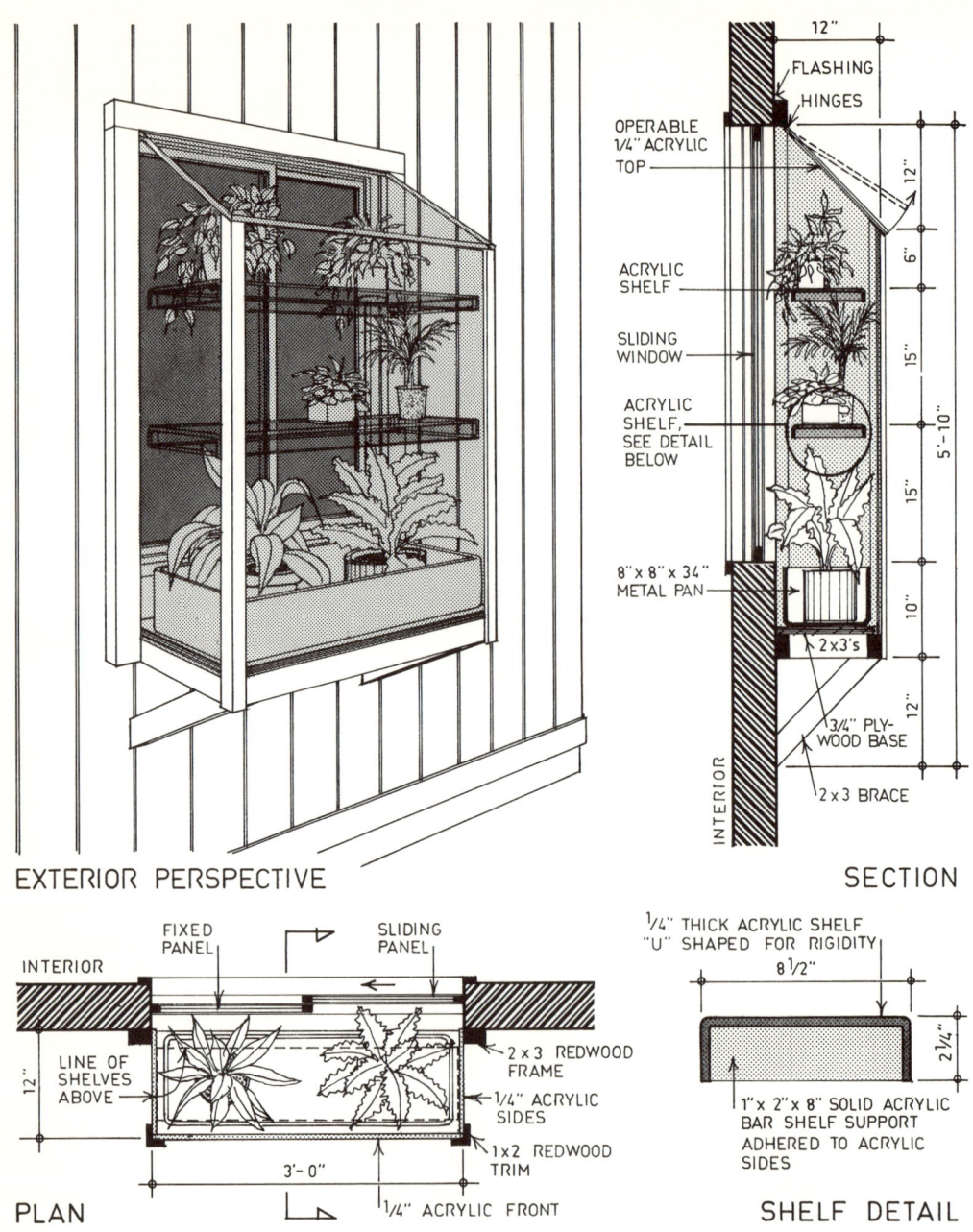

Acrylic Window Greenhouse

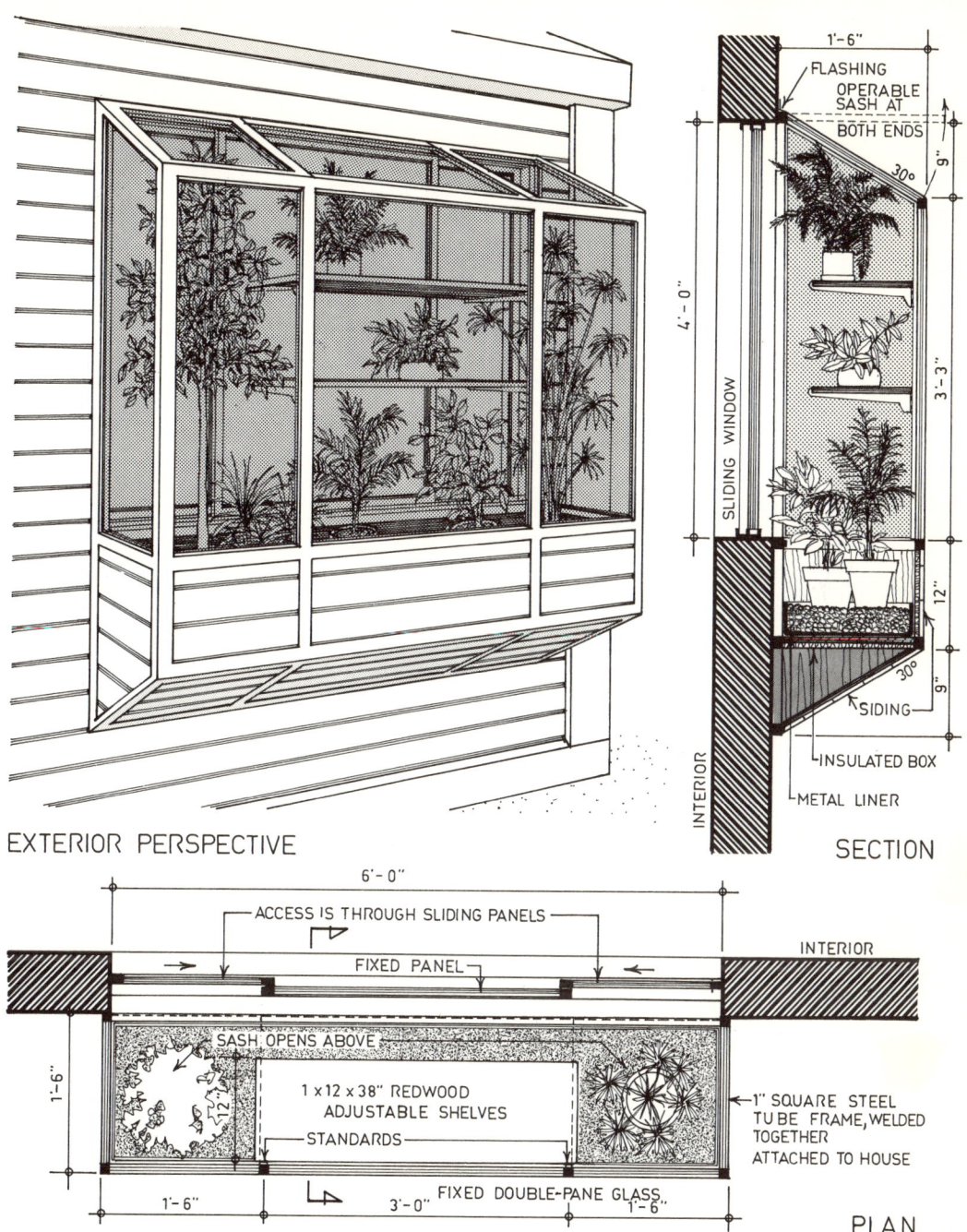

EXTERIOR PERSPECTIVE

SECTION

PLAN

Steel Frame Window Greenhouse

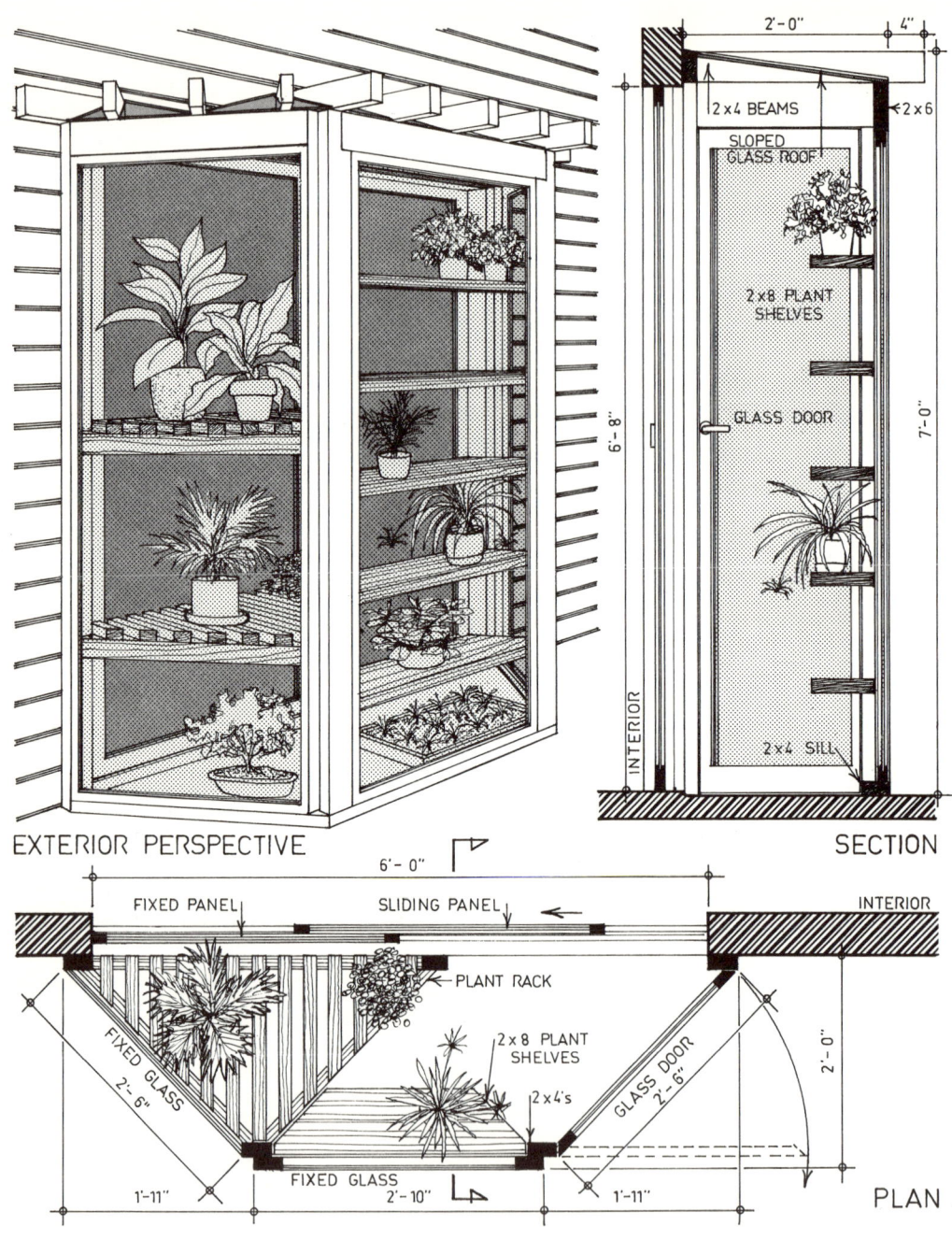

Bay Window Greenhouse

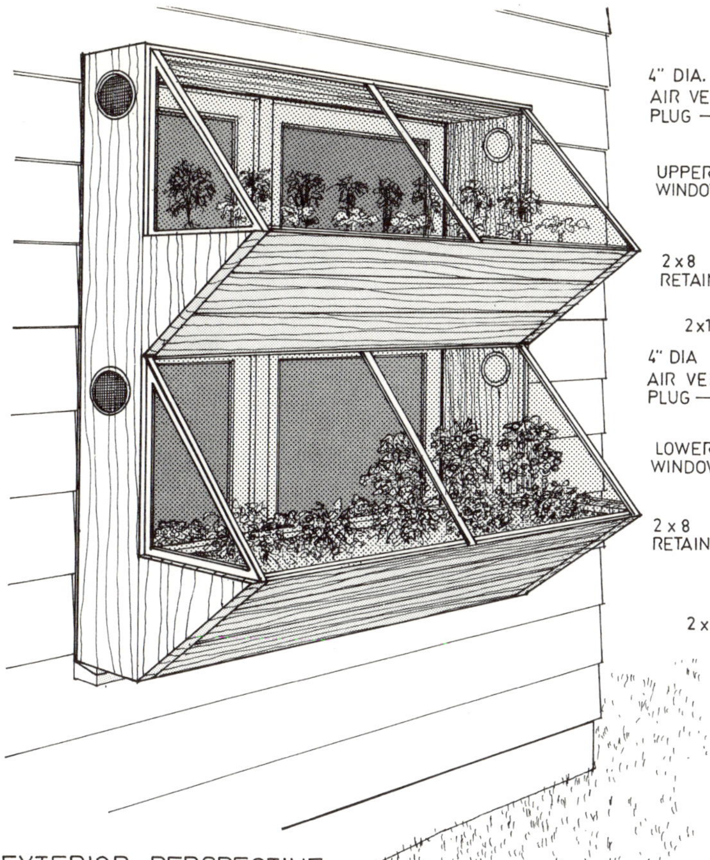

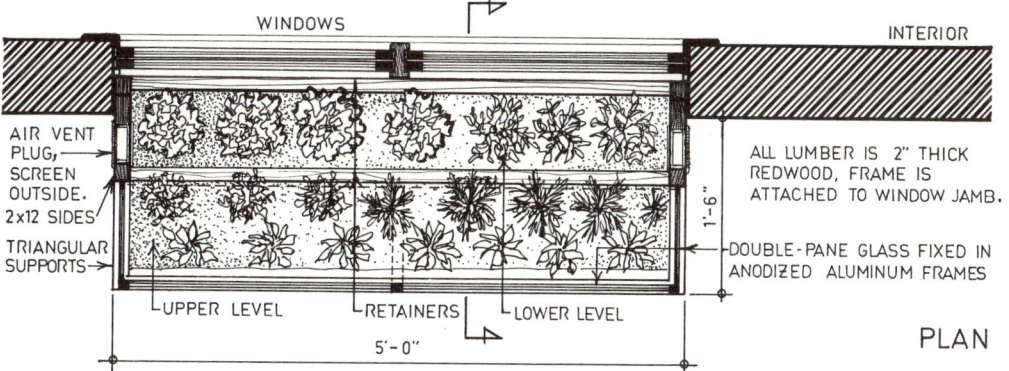

Saw-tooth Window Greenhouse

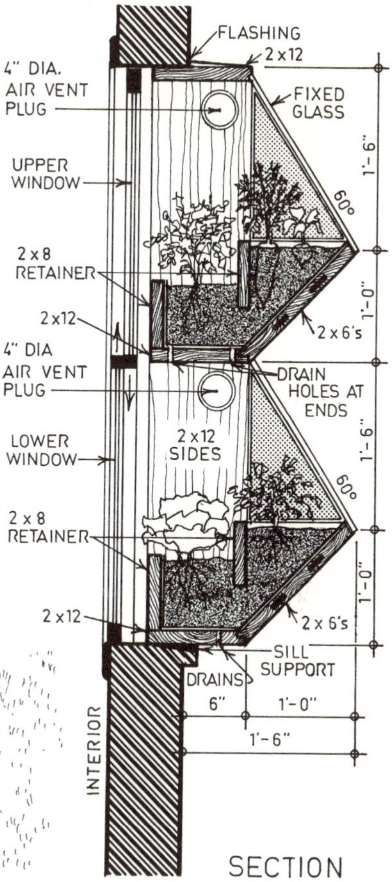

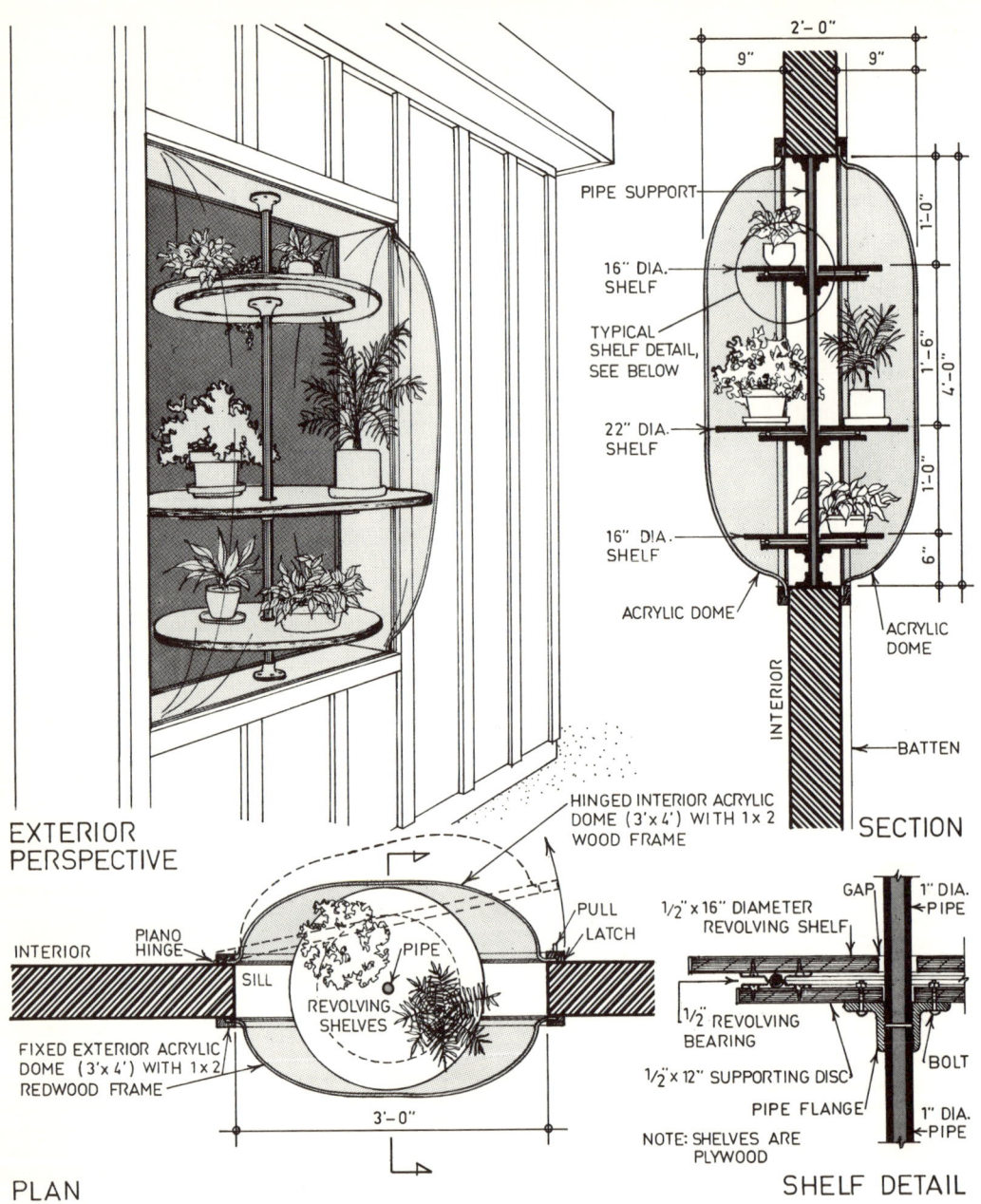

Double Acrylic Dome Window Greenhouse

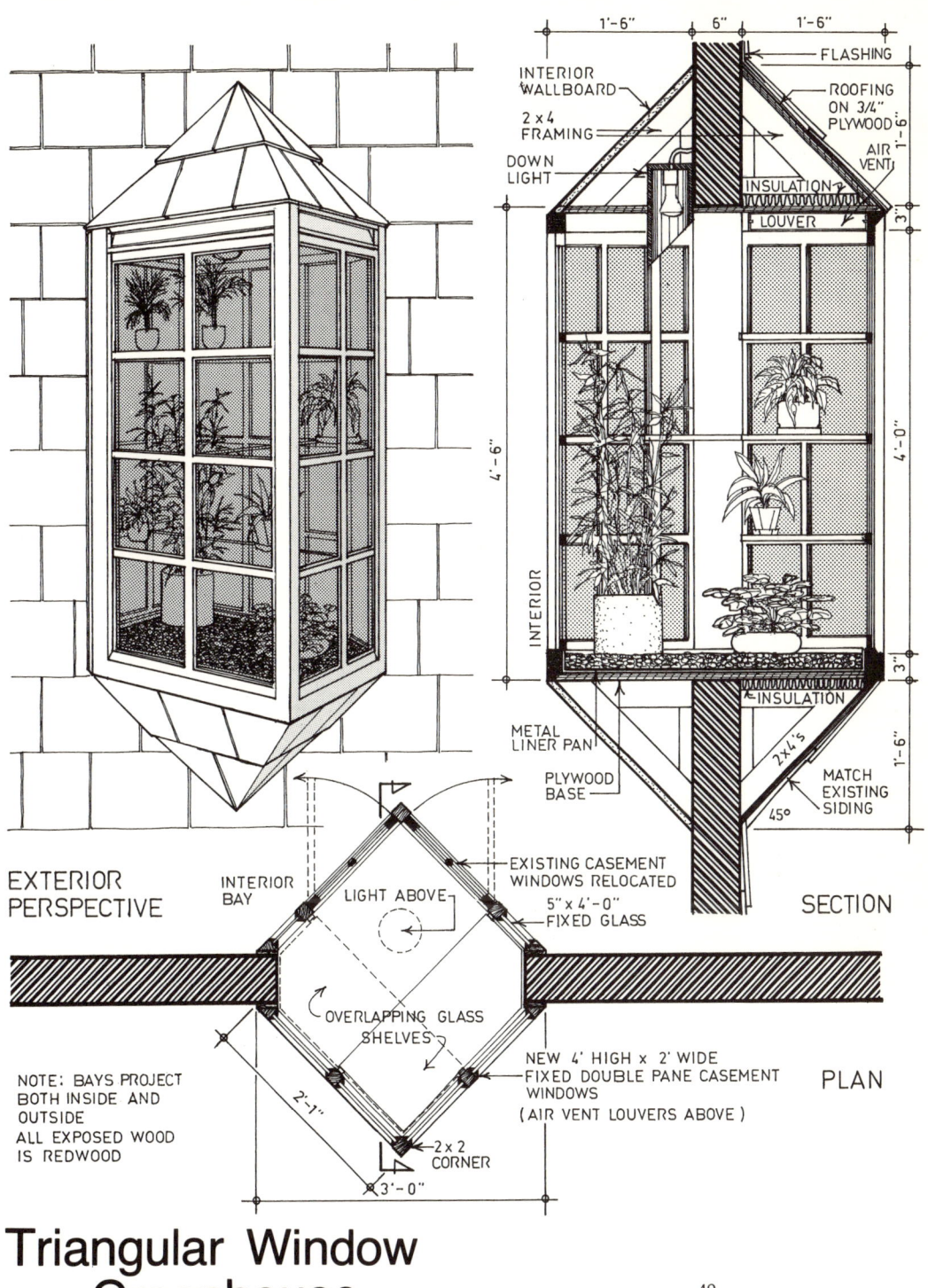

Triangular Window Greenhouse

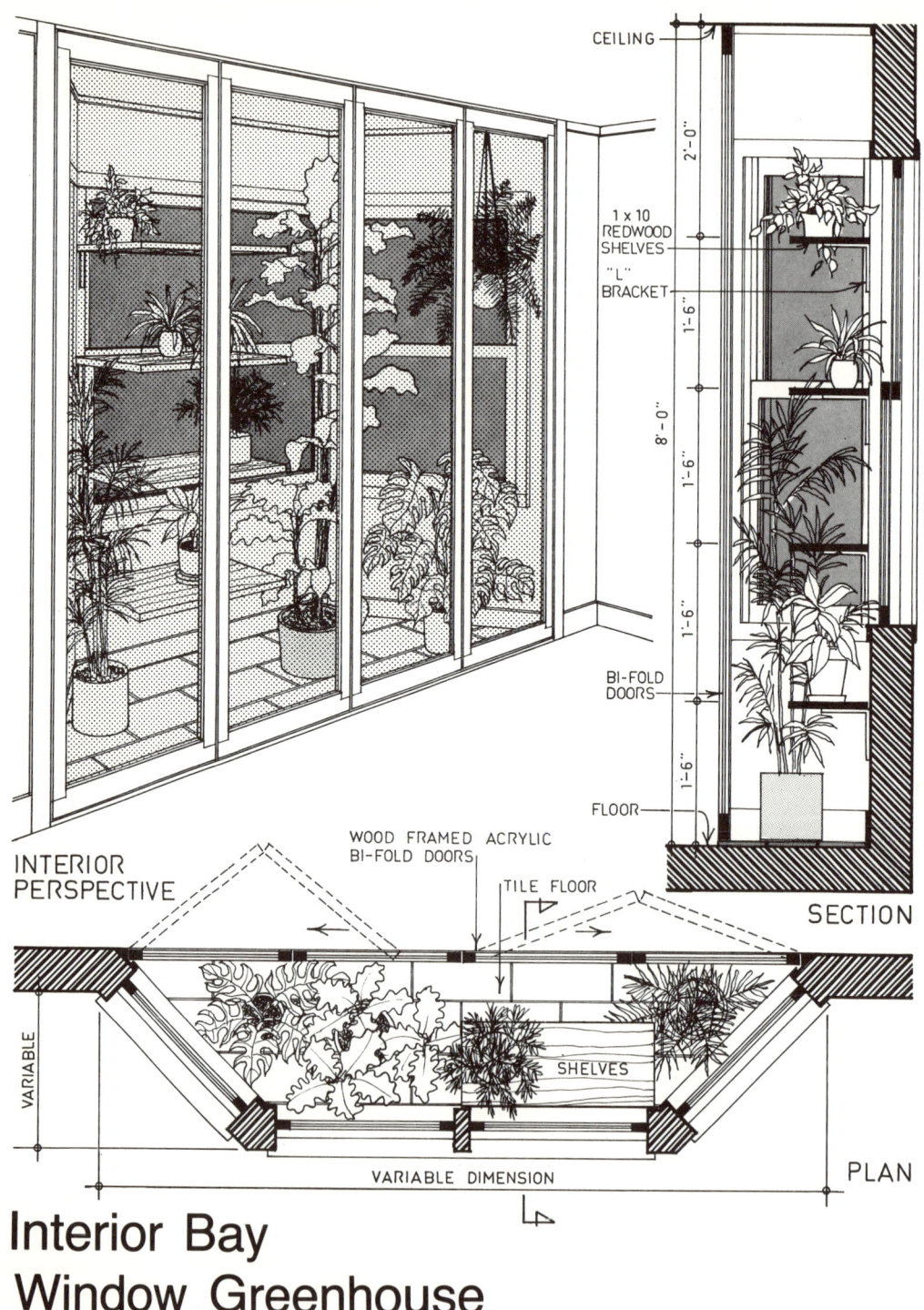

Interior Bay Window Greenhouse

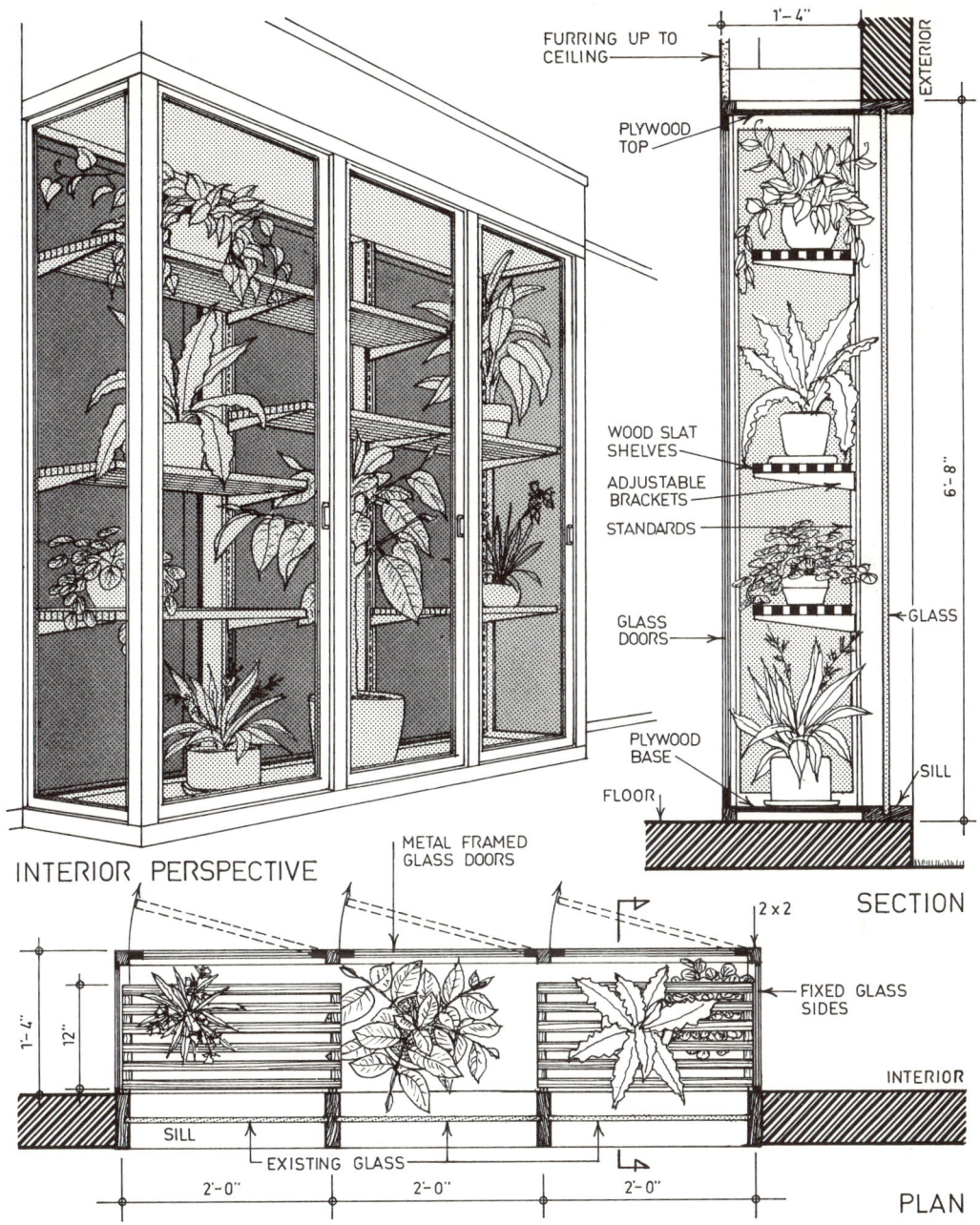

Interior Showcase Greenhouse

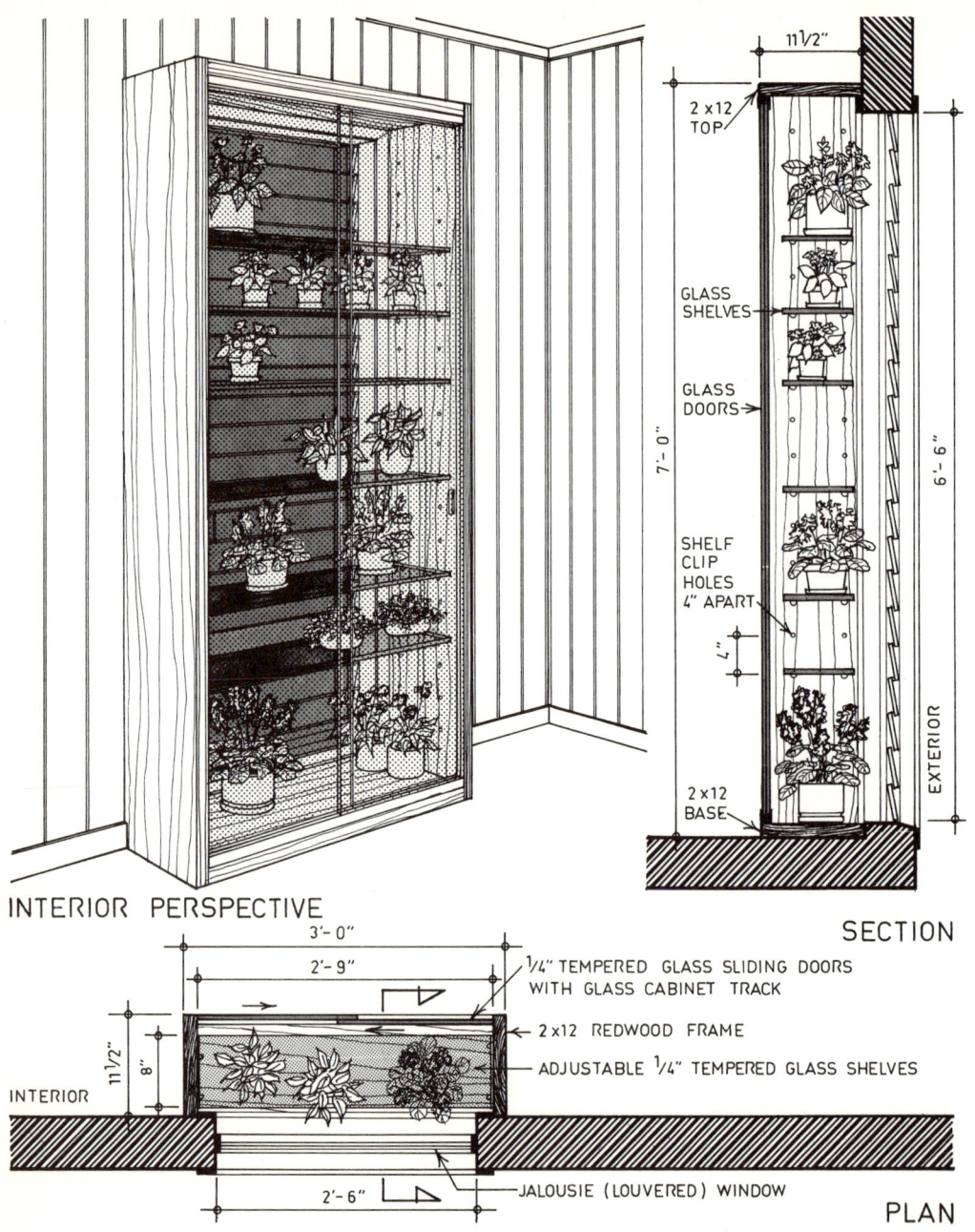

Interior Window Garden

52

4 Growing Conditions in the Window Greenhouse

Temperature, humidity, and ventilation conditions within the window greenhouse differ from conditions in the home. With the window closed you create a controlled environment, similar to a terrarium, in which your plants produce their own moisture. Also, the light in the greenhouse is better than light in a room. Factors such as these lead to a different set of cultural rules for plants in a window greenhouse than for those in a windowsill garden.

Light Exposure

Selection of plants for the window greenhouse should be considered in terms of the greenhouse's exposure. If your window faces east or south, there is sufficient light for almost any kind of plant, including vegetables and sun-loving annuals and perennials. A western exposure limits the choice somewhat more, but there are hundreds of species that will do better at this exposure because they prefer bright general light to direct sun. For a north window you have to pick and choose plants among those that specifically perform well in moderate or low light.

Since the light in an east or south window will be strong most of the year, in summer you will have to shade your plants from the sun's direct rays. If you do not shade them the leaves will turn brown or black from sun scorch. The lazy person's way of shading is to let the panes get dirty; the dust and soot provide a measure of protection against intense sunlight. However, this is hardly an ideal situation, especially if you want your greenhouse to look attractive, so use curtains within the greenhouse or hardware cloth (screening) against the outside to reduce intensity. At other exposures protective measures will not be necessary.

While we are talking about light, I want to mention that plants should be given a quarter turn once a week so all parts of the plant receive light evenly. Otherwise the plants may grow lopsided and lose their symmetrical shape.

Let's look at what you can grow at each exposure. Quite frankly, growing tomatoes in a north window will not work—but shade-loving orchids will. It is better to pick and choose your plants according to the exposure your window greenhouse has, so you'll enjoy pretty and healthy plants rather than waning ones. Success breeds success, and I want you to get started right.

Plants for East and South Windows

In an east or south location you can fill your greenhouse with an array of flowering plants that will brighten every day. Many of these plants are grown from bulbs. (Their descriptions are given in the next chapter.) Some orchids can be grown too, as well as bromeliads and begonias.

Most certainly try your hand at some annuals and perennials in a south or east greenhouse because they offer bright color and most of them, such as petunias, are very easy to grow. They will make your window greenhouse really look like an outside garden—especially valuable if you live in an apartment or house where there is little or no outdoor planting.

It is unfortunate that you will not have space for everything because in a sunny window you can also grow most of your vegetables (midget varieties). (These are described in chapter 6.) Selection will be vital as to what you want: flowers, vegetables, houseplants, and so forth. Try one type of plant one year and another the next; or perhaps install another window greenhouse.

Plants for West Windows

A west window is what you will want for begonias and gesneriads like African violets—where the sunlight is good but indirect. Plants such as campanulas as well as some orchids and many bromeliads will do fine here. Annuals and perennials will have sparse bloom if any, and you can grow only leafy vegetables such as spinach and lettuce, and possibly tomatoes.

Plants such as episcias and columneas like the weak rays of the western sun, as do oxalis and the peacock plant. Any of the foliage houseplants, such as dieffenbachias and dracaenas as well as philodendrons (described in chapter 5), will do fine in this location, and several kinds of herbs grow well too.

Plants for North Windows

The greenhouse in north light is the place for many popular houseplants that flourish under controlled conditions. This is the ideal location to grow ferns and philodendrons, and there are dozens to choose from. My favorites among the philodendrons are *Philodendron soderoi*, with heart-shaped leaves, and *P. wendlendi*, with a rosette shape. These do not take up as much space as many of the vining types.

Favorite houseplants such as dieffenbachias and dracaenas are other excellent candidates for the north window. These bold-leaved beauties want some light but little direct sun, so a north-facing greenhouse is ideal for them. You might also want to try exotic plants such as marantas, calatheas, and anthuriums that need the high humidity (60 percent) found in a greenhouse. Some of the smaller members of the ficus family such as *Ficus diversifolia* (mistletoe fig) are excellent at the north window, or try some small palms like *Rhapis excelsa* and *Livistonia*.

Don't put in vegetables—they just won't work; and of course flowering plants of the outdoor variety will have little bloom where there is minimum sun. Select foliage plants or some of the others mentioned above. Also remember that a north window greenhouse is an ideal place to rest bulbous plants during the winter months.

Watering

Because window greenhouse plants grow all year if they have sufficient light, your watering schedule will depend on the weather. For example, in a sunny year plants need more water than in a gray and dull year. Generally, plants in a window greenhouse need water every third day in spring and summer but only once a week in winter. If your plants have a northern or western exposure, water them slightly less—say, twice a week in spring and summer and once a week in winter.

Your watering schedule will also depend on the size of the pots. Plants in small pots (4 to 7 inches) dry out more quickly than plants in larger pots (8 to 18 inches), so exercise common sense and water larger plants less often.

When you water plants really wet them (being sure excess water runs out into drainage saucers). Spotty watering creates air pockets in the soil that can harm a plant—when roots hit the dry areas they just stop growing. Use a watering can large enough to water the entire window garden. Running to and from the kitchen sink with plants is foolish, so do buy a good can. My 2-gallon plastic can with a long nozzle waters about twenty plants in 8- to 10-inch pots. (Plastic cans are good, but brass ones are the best.)

Try to water your plants at a specific time of day, perhaps after your morning coffee or when you get home from work. Always use tepid water because cold water shocks plants. Do not worry about the quality of your water supply; if you can drink the water it is safe for your plants.

Once a month take the plants from the window greenhouse and soak them in a sinkful of water to within ½ inch of the pot rim. Leave them in the water for about an hour, or until you see air bubbles on the surface of the soil. This soaking eliminates toxic salts from the soil and brings to the surface any unwanted insects that may be hiding in the pot.

Soil

There are so many kinds of soil on the market that it is hard to determine just what to get. Do you buy standard packaged houseplant soil and plant everything in it? Or do you buy special soils? To simplify the problem, simply buy standard houseplant soil and add to it for different types of plants. For cacti and other succulents add 1 cup of sand to an 8-inch pot of soil (that is, 1 cup per cubic foot). For flowering plants add 1 cup of bone meal to an 8-inch pot. For annuals and perennials add ½ cup of compost and ½ cup of bone meal. For most standard foliage plants, like dieffenbachias and dracaenas, use the soil as it comes from the package. However, for vegetables and herbs make an exception: buy a special vegetable soil and add compost to it—generally, 1 cup to a 12-inch container.

The amount of soil you have to buy depends on how many plants you are growing. Most packaged soils come in 1-, 3-, or 5-cubic-foot bags. The 1-cubic-foot bag (called a hobby sack) contains enough soil for five 5-inch pots; the 3-cubic-foot bag contains enough for twelve 6-inch pots; and the large bag (which weighs about 50 pounds) usually will pot twenty or more plants. Buy the size most convenient for you. If you live in a three-flight walk-up, one or two hobby sacks at a time are the answer; but if you are at ground level, the large sack is the most economical, provided you can lift it. Hauling soil around is no joke, so do consider weight and package size.

What brand should you buy? I cannot say because there are so many. Generally, most packaged soils contain sufficient nutrients for your plants.

Soilless mixes are also available. These are lightweight but they contain no nutrients, so you must feed your plants continuously throughout the season, which can be a bother. What you save in weight you make up for in the additional cost of plant foods; but soilless mixes do have their uses and you might want to try them. If so, be sure to buy enough plant food.

Feeding

There are innumerable plant foods on the market, but I suggest you buy just *one* type. In other words, forget foods that are supposedly for specific plants like violets or citrus. I use a 10–10–5 fertilizer for all plants, and this has proved very satisfactory because it is neither too strong nor too weak. The numbers denote, successively, the proportions of nitrogen (for leaf growth), phosphorus (for healthy root growth), and potash (for resistance to disease). Thus a 10–10–5 food has 10 percent nitrogen, 10 percent phosphorus, and 5 percent potash.

The new time-release fertilizers supply plants with food over a 3-month period. One application does it. You can try these new products, though I am reluctant to do so because I never know just how much food is being released, and once started, the release process cannot be stopped. If I see signs of overfeeding—browning of leaves—I can always stop applying plant food, but if I am using a time-release preparation there is little I can do to help the plant. Also, some plants, like palms, react adversely to plant food, while others need only a little. Obviously, a time-release fertilizer is not for all plants.

General Feeding Rules

1. Never feed a newly potted plant—it does not need it.
2. Never feed an ailing plant.
3. Once every few months apply fish emulsion to help plants grow.
4. Never feed a dry plant.
5. Do not feed plants during the winter, when most plants rest.

If you repot plants yearly you will not have to use exorbitant amounts of plant food because fresh soil contains enough nutrients to keep a plant healthy and growing for many months.

Potting

Plants confined to containers use up nutrients in the soil in a matter of three to nine months. When this happens you must either provide plant food to furnish nutrients or, better yet, repot the plant in fresh soil—and use supplemental feeding only occasionally. Repotting a plant takes but a few minutes, but it must be done correctly to ensure that the plant will grow well.

To take a plant out of its pot, gently rap the edge of the pot against the edge of a table or workbench to loosen the root ball. Now firmly grasp the collar of the plant and jiggle it to detach the root ball from the inside surface. You want to remove the plant with as much of the soil as possible intact to lessen the shock of replanting.

If you cannot tease a plant out of an old pot, it may be because the roots have adhered to the inside surface. It is better to break the old pot with a hammer than to pull out the plant. Pulling will break off the roots, which will be quite a shock to the plant. Better to lose a dirty pot than a good plant.

Select a clean new container or scrub an old one with boiling water. Put a few pot shards (pieces of broken clay pots) at the bottom and insert a mound of soil. Center the plant on the mound; if it is too high remove some soil; if it is too low add some. Now fill in around the plant with more soil. Knock the bottom of the pot on a flat surface to settle the soil and then, with a blunt-edged stick or your thumbs, press the soil into the pot firmly around the collar of the plant. Add more soil to within ½ inch of the top of the pot and tamp it down again. You want the soil firmly but not tightly packed to eliminate any air pockets. Water the plant thoroughly; in an hour or so water it again. Then put it in the greenhouse.

5 Decorative Plants for the Window Greenhouse

Small- to medium-size plants are most appropriate for the window greenhouse because they are more in scale with the total scene. There are hundreds of miniature and slightly larger plants you can grow. In this chapter I'll describe some of the very good ones—those that may be a little more robust than others, and those that have a redeeming feature like handsome foliage or flowers. But these are certainly not all the plants you can grow; by all means if you have any particular favorites I have omitted, do grow them.

A window greenhouse can accommodate all kinds of plants. Here African violets, bromeliads, and orchids share space with caladiums and hydrangeas. (Photo by Jerry Bagger)

Miniatures

Many plant families—begonias, geraniums, orchids, gesneriads—include miniature varieties that rarely grow over 12 inches. These diminutive members are just as beautiful as their larger counterparts.

The requirements of the miniatures depend on the family they belong to. For example, gesneriads like a bright and somewhat moist place; some orchids require a sunny location. However, no miniature is difficult to grow once it becomes accustomed to its environment. This adjustment takes a few weeks, so do not panic if some plants lose a few leaves and others sulk a bit—eventually they'll recover and do just fine.

Because miniature plants are in small pots (3-, 4-, or 5-inch containers) they will need more frequent waterings than standard plants in larger pots. Otherwise follow the general cultural rules for the common plant group.

Cacti and Other Succulents

These plants offer a wealth of beauty that is often overlooked. Rebutias and parodias, only 2 to 4 inches tall, are handsome globular cacti that bear large flowers. Haworthias, equally attractive but with a rosette growth shape, are also desirable. And from the large group of crassulas there are many handsome species, such as *Crassula cooperi* and *C. schmidtii*.

Keep succulents evenly moist all year except in winter, when they should be grown almost dry (but never bone dry). Use a sandy soil; I add 1 cup of sand for a 12-inch pot of houseplant soil. Cacti and other succulents do fine in a bright or directly sunny greenhouse window. Do not feed these plants; you want them to stay small. An application of fish emulsion once every three months is fine.

Try these succulents for greenhouse growing:

Crassula argentea—green leaves edged red; branching habit.
C. cooperi—small, pointed leaves with dark markings.
C. schmidtii—pointed red-tinted leaves.
Echinocactus grusonii—golden yellow globe, yellow blooms.
E. horizonthalonius—silvery gray-and-pink leaves with red spines.
Echinocereus dasyacanthus—small, dense spines and yellow flowers.
E. reichenbachii—ribbed globe, white to red flowers.
E. rigidissimus—multicolored spines with pink, white, red, and brown flowers.
Echinopsis campylacantha—grayish green globe, purple-and-white blooms.
E. multiplex—dark green barrel shape; rose-colored flowers.
Gymnocalycium mihanovichii—grayish green globe, white flowers.
G. schickendantzii—white or pinkish white flowers.

Haworthia margaritifera—pointed leaves with white warts.
Kalanchoe blossfeldiana—red blooms at Christmas.
K. carnea—pink blooms.
Lobivia aurea—yellow flowers.
L. backebergii—red flowers.
Parodia aureispina—globe shape; large yellow flowers.
Rebutia kupperiana—scarlet flowers.
R. minuscula—scarlet flowers.
R. violaciflora—purple flowers.
Sedum adolphii—yellow-green bushy growth; white flowers.
S. dasyphyllum—blue-green rosette shape; pink blooms.
S. multiceps—shrubby growth; lovely yellow blooms.

Gesneriads

African violets are perhaps the best-known gesneriads, but there are many others that also make fine indoor plants. Columneas, episcias, and sinningias offer many excellent varieties for greenhouse growing. None of these plants require bright light—in fact, they do well in moderate light.

Pot gesneriads yearly in a rich, porous soil. These plants will not tolerate overwatering—gesneriads generally like to dry out between waterings. Feed plants in spring and summer with a weak solution of 10–10–5 plant food; not at all the rest of the year. Keep the air in the window greenhouse in circulation—gesneriads do not like stagnant conditions.

African Violet Varieties (Miniature)

'Bonanza'—ruffled red-violet flowers.
'Carita'—fine blue blooms.
'Fancy Doll'—dark-pink-and-white blossoms.
'Irish Elf'—frilled double white flowers.
'Little Mo'—bronzy red-violet foliage with green edges.
'Minikin'—double blue-and-white flowers.

Other Gesneriads

Columnea microphylla—tiny, hairy coppery leaves, red flowers.
Episcia dianthiflora—dark green leaves, white flowers.
Gloxinia—handsome leaves, large, tubular flowers in striking colors.
Hypocyrta nummularia—red hairy stems, small orange-yellow flowers.
H. radicans—shiny green leaves, orange-yellow blooms.
Kohleria amabilis—bell-shaped white flowers with purple throat.
Rechsteineria cardinalis—large, fuzzy green leaves, bright red flowers.
Sinningia 'Baby Doll'—an excellent miniature.
S. pusilla—orchid-colored blooms with darker veins and yellow throat; a miniature.
Streptocarpus rexii—lovely blue or mauve flowers.
S. sacorum—pale lilac flowers with white throat.

Begonias

Begonias comprise a vast plant family, with many small members that are resplendent at windows. There are many groups of begonias within the family—hirsute, rhizomatous, fibrous, and so forth. Most are stellar plants that do fine in the window greenhouse.

Many begonia varieties are shallow rooted, so do not use deep pots or the soil will turn sour from too much water and injure the plants. Use a light, humusy soil—add 1 cup of compost or humus per standard hobby sack of packaged soil. Give plants bright light, and in winter as much sun as possible. Feed plants only in spring and summer, using a weak solution of 10–10–5 plant food.

These are some of the small begonias I grow:

'Baby Perfectifolia'—deep green shiny, pointed leaves with chocolaty edge.
'Baby Rainbow'—green leaves with purple center and purplish brown margin suffused with carmine red; silver spotted.
Begonia albo-picta—small green, silver-spotted leaves, dark pink blossoms.
B. dregei—succulent red stems and thin, shallow-lobed leaves, bronzy green with purple veins; white flowers.
B. foliosa—a dainty, fernlike plant with drooping branches clothed in tiny, oblong leaves; showers of white flowers.

B. imperialis—emerald green leaves that are velvety and pebble textured; white flowers.

B. richardsiana—green leaves, white flowers.

B. weltoniensis—somewhat large handsome foliage.

'Berry Autumn'—leaves with reddish brown center and edge.

'Black Falcon'—black star-shaped leaves with wide silver marking outlining the veins; clusters of pink flowers.

'Bow Chance'—dark green leaves with light green veins; reddish brown stems; pink flowers.

'Bow Joe'—one of the daintiest; tiny, pointed black leaves, clusters of pink flowers.

'China Doll'—small, pointed light green leaves with wide brown veins and hairy edge, clusters of small pink flowers.

'Chantilly Lace'—chartreuse leaves with black edge.

'Lucy Closson'—small dark leaves flecked with silver and rose.

'Red Berry'—reddish brown leaves, of autumn hues.

'Rosa Kugel'—small, cupped green leaves, pink flowers.

'Spaulding'—brownish green on top of leaf and red underneath, with hairy margin; pink flowers.

Orchids

Orchids, the exotic beauties of the plant world, will astonish you with their stunning flowers. Orchids bloom seasonally—spring, summer, fall, or winter—and will bloom every year.

Grow orchids in fine grade fir bark (packages available at nurseries), never in soil, because orchids are mainly air plants. Give them bright light, and be sure the potting medium is evenly moist all year.

Some orchids need full sun to bloom, but most do fine with just bright light. The plants in the following list should bear flowers in moderate or bright light:

Angraecum compactum—3-inch white flowers, dark green straplike leaves.
Asocentrum ampullaceum—dark green leaves, erect spikes of cerise flowers.
A. miniatum—spikes of orange blooms, straplike dark green foliage.
Capanemia uliginosa—small, scented white flowers, solitary, cactuslike fleshy leaves.
Cattleya walkeriana—leathery green leaves, 3-inch rose-colored flowers.
Coelogyne orchracea—beautiful orange-and-white flowers make this easy-to-grow orchid ideal for the greenhouse, where it will provide color in summer.
Dendrobium pierardii—a handsome orchid that bears lovely lavender flowers on bare canes; needs a month's rest after flowering.
Epidendrum lindleyanum—leafy stems, lavender flowers in autumn.
E. polybulbon—leaves on a creeping rhizome, brown-yellow flowers.
E. porpax—tiny, oval green leaves, waxy brown-purple flowers.

Kerfersteinia gramineus—1-inch yellow-green flowers with brownish red spots.

Leptotes bicolor—succulent foliage, large white-stained, deep violet flowers.

Lycaste aromatica—leafy growth, bright yellow flowers scented cinnamon; needs almost bone dry rest after blooming.

Masdevallia lilliputana—rarely taller than 1 inch; red-and-yellow flowers.

M. schroederiana—dark green foliage, helmet-shaped deep red flowers with spurs.

Oncidium ampliatum—one of the large orchids, the "turtle orchid" grows up to 40 inches, with strap leaves and pseudobulbs shaped like turtle shells; bears long wands of delightful small yellow flowers.

Ornithocephalus bicornis—leathery leaves in rosette pattern, bell-shaped greenish white blooms; best grown on cork or tree-fiber board (available at orchid suppliers).

Platyclinis cornuta—solitary leaves, and white flowers on a short scape; best grown on cork or tree-fiber board.

P. filiformis (Dendrochilum filiforme)—grassy foliage, tiny yellow flowers.

Stelis ciliaris—tongue-shaped dark green leaves, tiny red blooms.

S. micrantha—tiny green-white flowers, 6-inch green foliage.

Bromeliads

It is always difficult to decide whether bromeliads should be discussed as foliage or flowering plants. Generally, most of them do bloom in a window greenhouse, but it is more the leaves that gain popularity for this plant group—which, perhaps above all others, offers a dazzling array of colored foliage. Some species have banded foliage, others striped, and the leaf color ranges widely from bright apple green to almost burgundy. To enhance their desirability, most bromeliads are medium-size plants and do not require too much space. But what makes them an absolute must for gardeners is the ease of growing them.

Use equal parts soil and fir bark for bromeliads. Keep them evenly moist, and the cups or vases of the plants filled with water all year. Sunlight will develop the leaves to their peak of color, but even in shade the plants will grow, if not so colorfully. Bromeliads require the constant temperatures and humidity found in the window greenhouse. All in all, they are a most desirable choice.

Here are some favorite bromeliads:

Aechmea chantini—dark green leaves and a stellar flower spike loaded with brightly colored bracts.
A. fasciata—a vase-shaped plant, somewhat smaller than the above, with gray-green leaves banded in silver and a handsome flower head of tiny blue blooms.

Guzmania lingulata—a rosette-shaped plant with apple green leaves and a star-shaped flower head—usually orange; many varieties, all handsome.

Neoregelia carolinae tricolor—a flat-growing rosette of variegated leaves, the center of which turns fiery red at bloom time; very striking.

Nidularium fulgens—rosette shape; brightly colored leaves and a cup of tiny flowers.

N. spectabilis—similar to *N. carolinae tricolor*, but with dark green leaves; easy to grow.

Vriesia carinata—apple green leaves in rosette form and a feathery red-and-yellow flower crown.

V. splendens (flaming sword)—similar to the above, but with a thrusting brilliant orange flower spike.

Foliage Plants

Foliage plants such as dieffenbachias and philodendrons grow handsomely in any window greenhouse—whether north, south, east, or west exposure. It is well to select the smaller ones that will not outgrow the window in a short time. You can have a permanent collection of leafy beauties, or you can simply put houseplants in the greenhouse to refresh them for a few months, returning them afterward to the home.

Most leafy plants do not need intense light. Keep the soil evenly moist, and feed plants a 10–10–5 plant food once every month in spring and summer.

There are so many foliage plants to grow that I can only scratch the surface here.

Philodendrons

With 250 species, the philodendron group offers many different sizes and shapes of leaves: small, medium, large, lance-shaped, heart-shaped, oval, serrated, scalloped. Philodendrons have dark green leaves that absorb light, so they can live a long time in shady areas where other plants would not survive. In nature philodendrons grow in shady, wet forests. A great number are climbing plants.

Philodendrons grow best in a porous soil composed equally of sand, peat moss, and rich loam, in a bright but not sunny location. Do not flood the plants but try to keep the soil evenly moist all year. Feed moderately—every other month through the warm months. After a while mature vining philodendrons will produce leaves smaller than those at the base. In most cases this is due to exhaustion of soil nutrients, so repot the plants. (Actually, most philodendrons will grow just as well in clear water as in soil.) Wipe leaves occasionally with a damp cloth to keep them shiny. Grow plants under average conditions: 65° to 75°F during the day, 15 degrees less at night (never below 55°).

Mail order houses list twenty-five kinds of philodendrons—species and new hybrids. Here are some standbys:

Philodendron andreanum—handsome arrow-shaped foliage; plants need moisture and warmth, grow large.
P. cordatum (*oxycardium*) (heart-leaf plant)—glossy green leaves; grows in water or soil.

P. hastatum variegatum—a new hybrid, with yellow-and-green leaves.

P. panduraeforme—scalloped olive green leaves; grows low.

P. pertusum—a tough, robust grower, with deeply lobed, heart-shaped leaves; a variegated form (yellow-and-green) also available.

P. soderoi—large or small forms, with mottled leaves and red stems.

P. squamiferum—unusual leaf design; a good accent.

P. verrucosum—exotic, satin sheen foliage makes this species outstanding; needs warmth and humidity.

P. wendlandii—a self-heading cabbage philodendron, with dense rosettes of waxy green tongue-shaped leaves; grows large.

Ferns

As a group, the ferns offer a dazzling array of foliage accent. There are some with lacy fronds, others with bold fronds; some are delicate, and many are fragile. Ferns grow naturally in shady, moist, and cool locations. In a window greenhouse ferns do best at northern or western exposures.

The selection of ferns is bewildering; one mail order house lists over forty types. The Boston fern is perhaps the most popular, but others, like the rabbit's-foot and bird's-nest, are just too good to miss. So do try some of these plants.

Grow ferns in filtered light, and give them a very porous soil of equal parts loam, leaf mold, and sand.

Ferns and begonias occupy most of the garden area in this window unit. (Photo by Matthew Barr)

Keep them moist but never soggy. I do not feed ferns because fertilizer can burn the leaf tips. In fact ferns seem to grow better without supplemental feeding.

Ferns should rest in winter, so then decrease moisture to the point where the soil is barely damp. Plants prefer to grow in small pots and to be disturbed as seldom as possible.

Here are some especially good ferns:

Adiantum cuneatum—an old favorite, with many varieties (including *A. cuneatum excelsum*, 'Goldelse,' 'Matador'), all tolerant of adverse conditions; dark green fronds.

A. hispidulum—a dwarf maidenhair fern; charming.

A. nidus (bird's-nest fern)—evergreen fronds; outstanding.

A. tenerum wrightii—a typical maidenhair, one of the best.

A. viviparum—very lacy fronds, which produce plantlets.

Blechnum brasiliense—low-growing, coarse fronds; different.

Davallia fejeensis (rabbit's-foot fern)—fine feathery foliage, hairy, creeping rootstalks; a curiosity.

Nephrolepis exaltata (sword fern)—long, pendant fronds; robust and easy to grow.

N. exaltata 'Fluffy Ruffles'—heavily ruffled; choice.

N. exaltata 'Verona'—lacy in appearance; compact growth.

Phyllitis scolopendrium—pale green wide fronds.

Platycerium bifurcatum (staghorn fern)—drooping fronds; grow on a cork or tree-fiber board.

P. pumila—upright fronds in a fan shape; grow on a cork or tree-fiber board.

Polypodium polycarpon (strap-leaf fern)—best grown on a cork or tree-fiber board.

Polystichum (*Aspidium tsus-simense*)—an ideal dwarf fern.

P. setosum—stiff, glossy green fronds; compact growth.

Pteris ensiformis 'Victoriae'—the species offers many forms; this one is silver-and-green.

Dracaenas

Dracaenas, with either plain green foliage or variegated leaves, are native mainly to the west coast of Africa, an area with much rainfall. The genus offers several plants that are extremely decorative. *Dracaena marginata* and *D. fragrans massangeana*, if shaped and trained properly, grow into handsome trees in a few years. (Once dracaenas get big you should move them to a room as specimen plants.)

Some dracaenas tolerate shade, but the variegated kinds need some bright light. Plant in a moisture-retentive soil of equal parts loam, peat moss, and fine sand. Keep the medium moist but never soggy. Repot dracaenas every year because they do not thrive for very long in the same container.

Although there are many species, the following dracaenas are especially suitable for greenhouse growing:

Dracaena deremensis longii—bright-striped green-and-white leaves on a central trunk.
D. deremensis warneckii—gray-and-green leaves; a good accent plant.
D. fragrans massangeana (corn plant)—cream-colored stripes on broad green leaves; grows somewhat like a palm from a central core.
D. godseffiana—green leaves spattered with yellow; bushy growth, small size.
D. marginata (decorator plant)—clusters of blade-shaped green leaves edged with red; branches when young.
D. sanderiana—gray-green, white-margined foliage.

Dieffenbachias

This is a very popular group of houseplants, but not as amenable to cultivation as, say, dracaenas or ferns. Most dieffenbachias have broad leaves growing on a central trunk. They come in solid green or—the more handsome species—with variegated leaves. A mature plant is an impressive sight.

Dieffenbachias require a porous soil; let them dry out between waterings. Keep plants out of drafts. Dieffenbachias do best in bright light, but intense sun can harm the foliage. The plants respond well in average greenhouse temperatures; they require occasional misting with tepid water to maintain humidity. Wipe leaves with a damp cloth to keep them clean and handsome.

A few choice dieffenbachias are:

Dieffenbachia amoena—a broad-leaved plant that grows in rosette shape; foliage is green-and-white.
D. godseffiana—abundant green leaves splotched with white; handsome.
D. splendens—velvety green foliage with distinct white markings; dramatic.

Annuals and Perennials

Annuals and perennials generally require a southern exposure because they need plenty of sun to bloom. An annual plant lives for one season—about three months—while perennials come back every year with bloom.

Plants in both groups require copious watering and a good rich soil.

Some annuals, such as petunias, can be started in spring in the window greenhouse, either from seed or as prestarts, to provide color all summer. Or these flowering gems can be started and then moved to the garden, if you have one, for future bloom.

To start seed, use a shallow container such as an azalea (red clay) pot or a wooden box. You will need a starting medium such as vermiculite or some other packaged mix (sold by suppliers). Seed of most species germinate in 2 to 3 weeks. (For more information see chapter 7.) When seedlings are a few inches high plant them in soil in separate pots or, if you have outdoor space, in the ground.

Seed for annuals and perennials are being started here in galvanized metal bins. Some of the seedlings will remain in the window greenhouse; others will be planted in the garden. Conditions within the greenhouse are ideal for seed sowing. (Photo by Jerry Bagger)

Here the annuals and perennials are shown after a few weeks' care—up and growing lavishly. (Photo by Jerry Bagger)

DECORATIVE PLANTS FOR THE WINDOW GREENHOUSE

Annuals

Ageratum houstonianum (ageratum, flossflower). This plant, in blue, white, and pink varieties, blooms from early summer to fall. Start in the greenhouse for later outdoor growing.

Althaea rosea (hollyhock). Neglected in recent years, hollyhocks are making a reappearance in gardens; I recommend them because they are so colorful and survive in practically any situation. They grow to 6 feet, with large flowers in a spectrum of colors: pink, rose, yellow, red, white. Though generally classed as a biennial, it's best to start hollyhocks fresh every year. Start plants in the greenhouse and transfer to the garden later.

Antirrhinum majus (snapdragon). This is a tall, stately annual with lovely flowers; there are just about all colors to choose from except blue. Plants will tolerate a shady place in the greenhouse but usually do best in sun.

Calendula officinalis (pot marigold, calendula). This well-known selection, good for either greenhouse or garden, has bright, round flowers in a variety of colors: orange, cream, or gold. Pot marigolds grow 12 to 24 inches tall and bloom all summer.

Callistephus chinensis (aster, China aster). The 1- to 3-foot plants have wiry stems and beautiful white to deep red flowers. Some varieties bloom early, others in midseason, and still others in fall. This is one of the best flowers for cutting, so do start some in the greenhouse.

Centaurea cyanus (bachelor's button, cornflower). Growing to a height of 2½ feet, this fine annual bears pink, white, wine, or blue flowers; the gray-green foliage makes a dramatic display. Plants require pinching and pruning but they bloom profusely.

Cobeae scandens. A sprawling vine, it is worth its space because of its large, cup-shaped purplish flowers.

Coleus blumei (coleus). This foliage plant comes in many varieties. The tapestry-colored, toothed leaves are an asset in any window greenhouse. Plants can reach 3 feet or more; pinch growing tips to make them compact.

Dianthus (pink, sweet william). There are so many varieties that it gets confusing, but do try these plants; they have fine pink or white flowers and are very floriferous.

Impatiens balsamina (impatiens). Get to know this annual —it is a stellar plant for the window greenhouse. Impatiens comes in many different colors and heights and blooms profusely. It likes some sun but also succeeds in shade.

Lobularia maritima (alyssum). Available in several colors, this fine low-growing annual can be cultivated all season in the window greenhouse from seed started at various times.

Phlox drummondii (phlox). Phlox has lovely clusters of 1-inch flowers, in rose, crimson, salmon, white, or scarlet. This handsome annual needs plenty of sun and water. Good in the outdoor garden, phlox can be started from seed in the greenhouse.

Senecio cruentus (cineraria). Here is an annual that will

bloom in a northerly greenhouse. The daisylike flowers come in light or dark shades of blue, purple, and magenta. Plants grow from 12 to 15 inches and have handsome foliage. Keep them shaded and moist.

Tagetes erecta (marigold). This all-time favorite grows quickly, comes in all sizes from 6 to 40 inches, and blooms constantly from summer through fall. The blossoms, in many shades of yellow, orange, dark red, and maroon, can be used by themselves for lovely accents or with other plantings. There are many types, some of them new. 'French Dwarf' grows to 18 inches, in a fine array of colors; 'African Dwarf' to 16 inches. Most marigolds need an evenly moist soil in a sunny place. Grow them either in the greenhouse or outdoors.

Tropaeolum majus (nasturtium). The underrated nasturtium can bring an immense wealth of color to a greenhouse, and easier plants to grow can't be found. Nasturtiums bloom from summer until winter. They come single- or double-flowered, in shades of yellow, orange, crimson, or pink or multicolored. Start some seed in the greenhouse and just let them go. Nasturtiums provide a lovely indoor accent.

Zinnia elegans (zinnia). This popular annual comes in many sizes, forms, and colors. The plants are infinitely suitable for gardens, so start some in the window greenhouse. They are fast growers that need plenty of water.

Perennials

Aster frikartii (aster) and *A. novae-angliae* (New England aster). Their dramatic blue or purple flowers make these two perennials outstanding. The daisylike blooms, produced in abundance, are bright and showy in either the greenhouse or the garden.

Astilbe japonica (false spirea). A perennial for shady places, this plant has white, pink, or red flowers on wiry stems. The bronze-green leaves are attractive. The bloom season is summer. False spirea grows to about 24 inches. A moist soil is essential.

Campanula persicifolia (bellflower). Bellflowers should be grown more often because they offer so much color. With their white or blue blooms in June and July, they form mounds of color up to 10 inches high. Give plants full sun or light shade, and be sure they're in well-drained soil.

Chrysanthemum maximum (chrysanthemum) and *C. morifolium* (Shasta daisy). These are available in a multitude of shapes: spoon, cushion, pompom, button. Colors vary from white to yellow, gold, or orange. Heights are variable, so there are forms for all kinds of locations. Plants will tolerate and even flourish in dry soil.

Delphinium elatum (delphinium, larkspur). This handsome tall plant develops spires of large flowers. Colors range from white to pink to superb blues. Rich, well-drained soil and sun are essential. *D. grandiflorum* (Chinese delphinium) is a magnificent relative.

Gaillardia aristata (blanketflower). Gaillardias produce showy flowers over a long period of time. The daisylike blooms are generally bright yellow, although bronzy scarlet types have been introduced. Though undemanding, the plants do best in a slightly sandy soil with adequate sun.

Gypsophila paniculata (baby's breath). The dainty, lacy plants grow rapidly to 2 feet and bear small, round white flowers in masses. Blooms last over a month if kept in the window greenhouse.

Papaver orientale (Oriental poppy). Oriental poppies are coming into popularity again, and it's difficult to find more dramatic flowers than their bold orange blooms. Plants are 2 to 4 feet high; once established, they produce 6- to 8-inch flowers profusely. They need well-drained soil and some (not direct or intense) sun.

Other Plants

Here is a sampling of some other decorative plants that will thrive in a window greenhouse. Some of these flowering species need at least 3 hours of sun daily to bear their colorful harvest, so use a south or east window for them.

Use a rich, porous soil—add 1 cup of humus or

A window greenhouse adds beauty to any home, creating a colorful scene that can be enjoyed from both inside and outside. (Photo by Matthew Barr)

compost and 2 tablespoons of bone meal for each standard hobby sack of houseplant soil. Keep the soil evenly moist all year, but feed plants scantily because too much plant food may force foliage growth at the expense of flowers.

Here are some exceptionally fine plants:

Allium neopolitanum (flowering onion)—a bulbous plant that bears a magnificent cluster of bright lavender flowers; rest in winter with scanty watering.

Allophytum mexicanum—with dark green leaves and fragrant, tubular lavender flowers, this is a nice addition to the window greenhouse.

Anthurium scherzerianum (flamingo flower)—handsome dark green foliage, bright red flower spathes; likes heat and high humidity.

Aphelandra chamoissiana—a leafy plant with a brilliant head of bright yellow flowers; very showy but difficult to grow.

Bougainvillea—not really ideal for the window greenhouse because it grows so large, but can be pruned to size if you want this brightly colored blossoming plant.

Campanula fragilis—small leaves growing in a halo shape, lovely bright blue star-shaped flowers; likes moisture and coolness.

Eucomis punctata (pineapple lily)—an unusual bulbous plant that bears handsome crowns of flowers in summer; in winter keep semidormant—almost dry (best moved out of the greenhouse to a shady area).

Haemanthus coccineus (blood lily)—an ornamental bulbous plant with fleshy leaves and a spherical head of hundreds of tiny flowers; after blooming and when foliage matures, remove from the greenhouse and rest almost dry for several months in the basement or garage (out of light).

Hedychium coronarium (ginger lily)—with lovely green glossy leaves and fragrant white flowers, this plant is worth its space even for its scent alone; does well in a greenhouse situation.

Hoya carnosa (wax plant)—oval leaves on vining growth (needing support), clusters of stunning white highly scented flowers; only mature plants bloom.

Lantana montevidensis—a cascading lantana with fine purple flowers for winter greenhouse display; likes coolness.

Petrea volubilis (queen wreath)—this vining plant will take up space in the greenhouse, but it's worth it for its magnificent blue flowers.

Rosa chinensis minima—these miniature roses make lovely, space-saving greenhouse subjects (there are many varieties); for the collector.

Ruellia macrantha—a fine leafy plant with bright cerise flowers in winter; nice accent for the greenhouse and easy to grow.

Schizocentron elegans (Spanish shawl)—one of the prettiest greenhouse plants you can have, with tiny green leaves and masses of lavender flowers in spring and summer; ideally low growing.

Sprekelia formosissima (Jacobean lily)—spectacular red flowers appear in June before the foliage; decrease watering somewhat in late fall and winter.

Thunbergia alata (black-eyed Susan)—a pretty outdoor flowering plant suitable for the greenhouse; flowers are orange with black center.

6
Food Plants for the Window Greenhouse

You might want to grow some vegetables and herbs, to cut down on your food bills. In the window greenhouse you can certainly try some midget varieties of eggplant, tomatoes, and cucumbers. You can also quite successfully grow lettuce in hanging baskets. Herbs are fun to grow, to season food or simply for their pleasant scent.

Vegetables

Vegetables must grow fast and continuously to provide the succulent freshness associated with home-grown produce, so be prepared to water, and water, and water them. Grow vegetables in a sunny window because they

In this greenhouse vegetable seedlings share the window with houseplants. The controlled conditions ensure good growth. (Photo by Jerry Bagger)

A close-up of vegetable seedlings: pepper, lettuce, and tomatoes. (Photo by Jerry Bagger)

need at least 5 hours of good light daily. You can start radish, carrot, and lettuce seed yourself, but for other vegetables I recommend that you buy prestarted plants (seasonally at nurseries).

Plant vegetables in containers—trays or pots—that are at least 10 inches deep; most need a very rich, porous soil. Add 1 cup of compost per standard package of houseplant mix, or buy one of the special vegetable soil mixes. Fertilize with standard vegetable foods, and harvest plants quickly when they are ready.

Beets

Beets are generally easy to grow. You can also eat the cooked greens. Plant seed 1 inch apart in containers about 16 inches deep and give them lots of water, keeping the soil evenly moist. Thin the plants as they start to grow. Beets prefer a moderate temperature (75°F).

Harvest beets when they are young and tender; they get pithy if left in the soil too long. Good varieties are 'Detroit Dark Red' and 'Ruby Queen.'

Carrots

Grow carrots in a long, somewhat deep planter. Use a porous soil mix—add 2 tablespoons of sand per standard package of soil. Scatter seed and cover them with ½ inch of soil. When tops show, thin the plants to about 2 inches; in a few weeks thin them again to 4 inches.

Harvest carrots as soon as they mature. If left in the soil too long they get pithy and lose their flavor. 'Little

Finger' and 'Gold Pak' are exceptional midget varieties. You will have a crop 70 days after starting seed.

Cucumbers

Cucumber vines are handsome—they resemble large-leaved ivy—and they produce a bountiful crop. There are dozens of varieties of cucumbers, some smooth skinned, some warty, some tiny, some large. These plants like heat and plenty of water. Plant prestarts in a rich soil in an 8-inch pot (add 1 tablespoon of rotted manure). Put a wooden trellis in the pot, and train the vines by tying them with string. Keep the soil evenly moist.

You should have cucumbers within 50 days. Pick them as soon as they are ready; if they are left on the vine, the plants will not continue to produce fruit. Two good midget varieties are 'Tiny Dill Cuke' and 'Patio Pik.'

Eggplant

The small, bushy eggplant makes a decorative effect in the window greenhouse. This warm-season vegetable does best at 80°F by day and 70°F at night. Buy prestarts; it takes seed months to germinate. Plant the prestarts in large tubs or in bins at least 20 inches deep. Eggplant needs even moisture at the roots and good sun.

Pick fruits when they are young (about two thirds their mature size) and their skins glossy. Harvest with shears; do not tear off the fruits. Good varieties include 'Black Beauty' and 'Japanese Hybrid.'

Lettuce

Lettuce is a stellar window greenhouse crop. Start seed in 8- or 12-inch clay pots in early spring before it gets too hot because lettuce is a cool-season crop. Keep soil evenly moist but never soggy.

Pick the outer leaves successively for several weeks, or just pick the entire head. There are several types of lettuce, including head, butterhead, leaf, romaine, and bibb. 'Butter Crunch' matures in 65 days; loose-leaf varieties like 'Oakleaf' and 'Salad Bowl' in about 50 days. 'Summer Bibb' and 'Big Boston' are excellent bibb-type varieties.

Peppers

Peppers make fine upright plants, and midget varieties produce 4- or 5-inch fruits, at least a dozen to a plant—more than enough for a family. Peppers need hot weather, but not above 90°F or they will not set fruit. For best results, try to keep the greenhouse at about 78°F. Plant two prestarts per 12-inch tub; use a rich soil laced with compost. Keep the soil evenly moist, and provide a buoyant atmosphere. Feed plants with fish emulsion when the first blossoms open.

Plants will bear within 70 days. To encourage more fruit, keep picking the peppers as they mature, when they are firm and crisp. (You can pick them green, or let them turn red on the plant.) There are hot and sweet peppers. Two good sweet pepper varieties are 'Bell Boy Hybrid' and 'Burpee's Fordhook.'

Spinach

A vegetable that likes coolness (70°F), spinach can be grown in your window greenhouse in early spring or late fall. (In hot weather spinach quickly goes to seed.) Plant seed ½ inch deep and 2 inches apart. Thin the seedlings to about 6 inches. Because spinach is a heavy feeder give plants fish emulsion a few times throughout the growing season.

Spinach matures in about 50 days. Harvest when the outer leaves are full size; if you pick just the outer leaves the inner ones will become the next crop. Good varieties include 'America' and 'Winter Bloomsdale.'

Tomatoes

Here are the favorites of the vegetable world (although tomatoes are actually a fruit). Tomatoes are a warm-season crop and need lots of sun and heat to prosper. Plant prestarts in large tubs in a rich, porous soil (two or three prestarts to a tub) and keep them evenly moist.

You can use Blossom Set on your tomato plants to be sure of harvest, or just shake the plants to get them pollinated. Tomatoes set fruit in a narrow temperature range: night temperatures must be between 60° and 70°F. Use standard tomato fertilizer once plants are growing.

There are dozens of tomato varieties, but I prefer the midgets 'Red Cherry,' 'Tiny Tim,' and 'Patio Pik.'

Herbs

There are dozens of herbs you can grow in a kitchen window greenhouse to provide you with seasonings all year. And growing your own herbs, from seed or pre-starts, saves acres of money—packaged herbs are very expensive.

Herbs are easy to grow in a somewhat sandy soil; use 1 cup of sand per standard package of soil mix. Keep plants well watered and sunny. Herbs are either annuals or perennials.

Basil

There are many types of basil, from the wide-leaved kinds to the coppery ones, but most people plant sweet basil. Sweet basil, which grows to about 24 inches, needs really strong sun to do its best.

Dill

You can do more with this annual herb than you may think. For instance, add dried dill when you boil artichokes for a pleasant taste treat. Dill is feathery and ferny in appearance; its only drawback is that it grows tall. The small yellow flowers bloom in clusters. Whenever the weather is warm you can sow seed of dill in the greenhouse. It will tolerate some shade if necessary.

Marjoram

This is one of my favorite herbs. I use marjoram in salads and fish dishes and with some meats. This is a perennial plant that generally lives over, but I find it just as easy to seed marjoram each year in trays in the greenhouse.

Parsley

With the price of parsley now at unheard-of levels, it makes good sense to grow your own in the greenhouse. And what a joy freshly washed parsley is to munch, let alone to cook with. Try to get the plain-leaved parsley rather than the curly-leaved; the curly-leaved type looks prettier, but plain-leaved parsley seems to have more flavor. This is a biennial—it comes back the second year after seeding. Parsley requires a constantly moist bed for germination, so it is best started in the greenhouse in trays. Plants will grow in bright light without much direct sun if they have to, but the more sun they get the better.

Rosemary

If you have space, grow some rosemary because it is good in fish dishes and as a medicinal herb as well. Seedlings root easily. The plants grow to about 36 inches; there are both upright and creeping varieties.

Sage

This perennial has gray-green leaves and pretty purple-and-white flowers. Plants need a sunny window. Sage is ideal for poultry stuffing.

Savory

Savory comes in two varieties—summer and winter. Summer savory is a delicate-looking plant with a few leaves; winter savory grows big, with dark green leaves and pretty white flowers. Both winter and summer savory will need sun. Both types are good for vegetable dishes and for poultry stuffing.

Tarragon

Get the right species of tarragon: *Artelisia dracunculus*. My best tarragon grows in a somewhat shady place in the greenhouse, although most herb experts say it does better in full sun—so try both ways and see. The herb is good in vinegars and in a sauce with white wine and butter for liver or fish.

Thyme

There are several varieties of this perennial, so try a few. If you give the plants sun they will grow by themselves. Thyme is good in egg dishes.

7 Starting New Plants in the Window Greenhouse

As we have seen, a window greenhouse can have many uses—for houseplants, for vegetables, for herbs. It can also serve as a place to start seed and cuttings of plants. The controlled humidity in the greenhouse makes it an ideal place for propagating plants and thereby saving money. Sowing seed is easy, and taking cuttings is fun. Indeed, starting plants is in itself an exciting adventure, and there is no better place to do it than in a window greenhouse.

Sowing Seed

Seed of many houseplants are available for spring starting, and you can also start vegetables—either to raise in

DIVISION

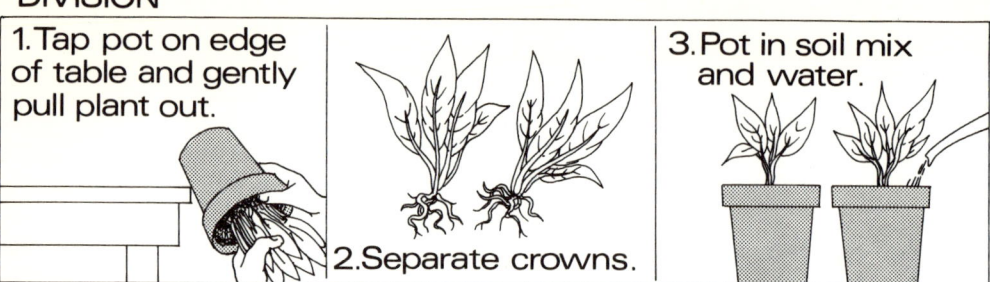

1. Tap pot on edge of table and gently pull plant out.
2. Separate crowns.
3. Pot in soil mix and water.

CUTTINGS

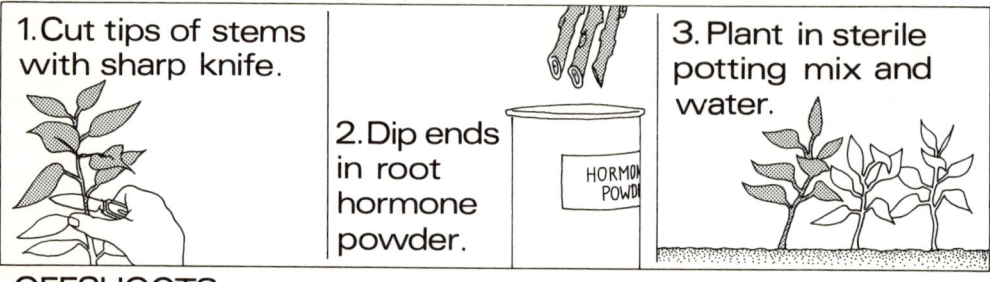

1. Cut tips of stems with sharp knife.
2. Dip ends in root hormone powder.
3. Plant in sterile potting mix and water.

OFFSHOOTS

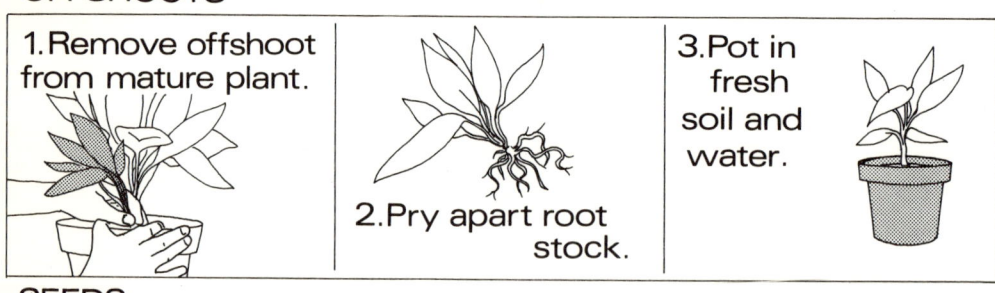

1. Remove offshoot from mature plant.
2. Pry apart root stock.
3. Pot in fresh soil and water.

SEEDS

1. Fill with sterile potting mix.
2. Sow seeds according to directions.
3. Keep plants moist.

Starting New Plants

the greenhouse or for outdoor planting later, if you have a garden. You can start annual and perennial seed for flowers too. The proper conditions for sowing seed are the same for most plants: warmth (about 75°F), enough humidity (about 60 percent), and good ventilation. Intense sun is not necessary—bright indirect light is fine.

To start seed you will need suitable containers and a sterile growing medium. The containers can be plastic trays, shallow wooden boxes, or any receptacles that will hold 3 to 4 inches of starting medium. Drainage holes are necessary so water can escape from the container rather than stagnating. You can also use standard clay pots or household containers such as the cartons frozen rolls come in. For the starting mix use any of the packaged types, such as vermiculite or one of the trade name brands.

Fill the container with growing medium to ¼ inch of the top and then sow the seed. Fine seed should be scattered on top, spaced about 2 to 4 inches apart, and larger seed should be imbedded slightly in the starting mix. Keep the mix evenly moist; a spray of water is usually better than just dumping water on the surface, which may disturb the seed.

Be sure correct humidity is maintained in the greenhouse. A constant 75°F can be approximated by opening and closing the greenhouse window.

You can also start seed in special growing mediums such as Jiffy Pellets or peat cubes (sold under various trade names). However, you will still need a container—a shallow box or tray—for these starters. Their advantage is that when transplanting time comes they can be planted along with the seedling, minimizing the shock to the plant.

Germination time—how long it takes for seed to sprout and leaves to grow—varies with each species, but usually growth starts in 2 to 4 weeks. Don't start feeding plants until they are up several inches. For more information on planting, see *Grow Your Own Plants* by Jack Kramer (Scribner's, 1975).

Taking Cuttings

If you don't want to spend the time starting seed, you can take cuttings of plants and start them in the window greenhouse. Some people start cuttings in plain water in a jar, but it is best to put them in a starting mix, as for seed. To take a cutting, cut the top 4 inches of a healthy stem. Remove the bottom two leaves—but allow three or four other leaves to remain—and insert the cutting in the starting mix in a box or tray. It is a good idea first to dip the end of the cutting in Rootone (available at nurseries) to stimulate root action.

When the cuttings have developed roots—and this varies in time for each species—they can be potted in fresh soil as new plants. After 3 or 4 weeks furnish them with some additional plant food.

Leaf Cuttings

This is an interesting way to propagate plants. You merely take a leaf and part of the stem and insert the leaf about half its length in a starting mix. Houseplants such as African violets and begonias are easily propagated by this method. Use shallow boxes or trays, as for seed sowing, and any general starting mix.

An alternative to imbedding the leaf is to cut a large vein on the undersurface of the leaf with a sterile razor blade; make a partial cut. Then place the leaf flat against the propagating mix with its natural upper surface exposed. (Be sure the leaf is in contact with the mix.)

Give the cuttings shade and high humidity in the window greenhouse. A new plantlet will form where each stem or vein was cut. When the new plants are a few inches high, gently remove them and place them in pots of soil.

8
Insects and Diseases

Plants in your window greenhouse may be attacked occasionally by pests such as aphids, mealybugs, or red spider mites. But none of these insects are particularly damaging *if* they are caught before they get a foothold. Insects spread rapidly, so it is especially important when growing groups of plants to eliminate insects as soon as you see them. Do not wait—mealybugs, for example, can produce 300 young in a day! Because your window greenhouse is at eye level and a part of your home, you will be seeing your plants frequently at close range, so spotting insects is easier than in an outdoor garden.

You can eliminate insects with either old-fashioned remedies or chemical pesticides. I object to poisons in the home, so I concentrate here on the old-fashioned

INSECTS AND DISEASES

methods. Whatever remedies you use, do know first what you are fighting. Diseases rarely bother indoor plants; however, these are also covered briefly.

Aphids

A plant infested with tiny aphids (plant lice) loses vigor and becomes stunted; leaves curl or pucker. Aphids are pear-shaped, small, soft-bodied insects with a beak that has needlelike stylets, used to pierce plant tissue and suck out the sap.

Mealybugs

Mealybugs have segmented soft, cottony bodies. The young are crawling, oval, light yellow insects with smooth bodies and beaks they insert into plant parts to get sap. Once they start feeding, the youngsters develop the typical cottony covering.

Red Spider Mites

These tiny, oval creatures are red, yellow, green, or brown; they have long legs. Although almost impossible to see on a plant, they do spin webs, which often give

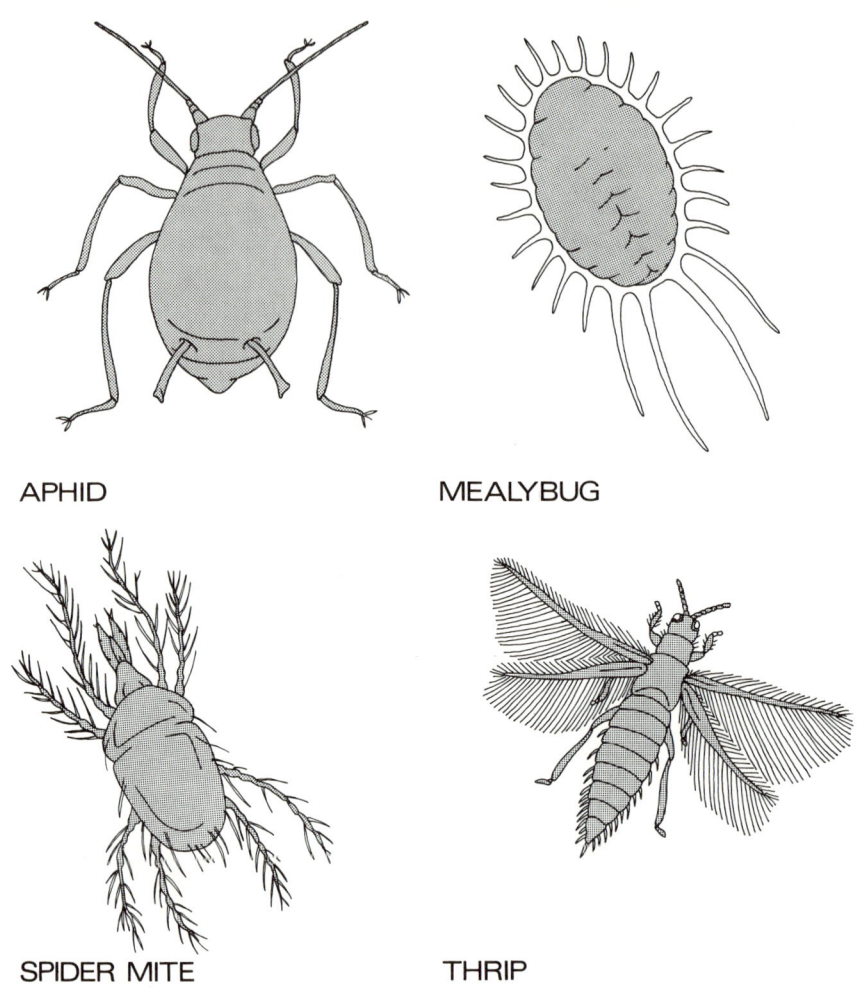

Common Insects

INSECTS AND DISEASES

them away. Mites injure plants by sucking out the liquid content of cells; foliage turns pale and may become stippled around the injured parts. Plants may become covered with the silken webs that the mites make as they move from area to area.

Scale

Scale are tiny, oval (but noticeable) insects with an armored shell covering their bodies. They insert their mouth parts in a leaf and start taking in sap. They stay in the same place throughout their lives. Plants infested with scale show stem as well as leaf damage. Of all the insects mentioned here, scale are the easiest to combat because they are so easily recognized.

Thrips

Thrips are chewing, very small, slender insects with two pairs of long, narrow wings. Adults are usually dark colored and appear in spring or summer. Some thrips are active flyers, others sort of jump around, and still others do not move much at all. Thrips leave a silver sheen on leaves.

Old-Fashioned Pest Remedies

There are several traditional, nonpoisonous ways of killing insects. These remedies may require more time because they generally have to be applied several times at weekly intervals, but I think they are worth the trouble, especially in home gardening.

Alcohol Swabs

Standard rubbing alcohol will control mealybugs and aphids. Dip cotton swabs in alcohol and apply to plants twice a week. Douse the insect, then spray it with water.

Nicotine

This is a rather good lethal way of getting rid of aphids and mealybugs as well as scale. Remove tobacco from cigarette butts and steep in 1 cup of water in a jar for several days. Then apply the solution with a cotton swab to the insects. Repeat every third day until insects are gone.

Soap and Water

Use 1 quart of water to a half bar of laundry soap (not detergent); a bar of facial soap can also be used. This mixture eliminates aphids and mealybugs.

Water Spray

This is more effective than most people may think. Use the strong-spray fixture at the sink, directing the spray at leaf axils and under leaves. This procedure eliminates many insects and their eggs. Repeat at weekly intervals.

Ground Pepper

Apply household ground pepper to the soil around plants to eliminate crawling insects.

Beer

Put out shallow dishes of beer to snare any slugs or snails that may invade the greenhouse.

Boiling Water

Pour boiling water on the soil to eliminate thrips. This may not kill the insects, but it discourages them.

Chemical Preventatives

Chemical insecticides can be either water soluble (applied to the plants with special sprayers), powdered, or granulated. The granulated systemics are perhaps the easiest to apply. The granules are spread on the soil,

INSECTS AND DISEASES

which is then thoroughly watered. The chemical is drawn up through the roots into the sap stream, making it toxic. Thus when sucking or chewing insects start dining on the plant they are poisoned. Systemics protect plants from most (but not all) sucking and chewing pests for 6 to 8 weeks, so they need be applied only three or four times a year.

How to Use Chemicals

In most cases repeated doses will be necessary to fully eliminate insects. Make sure you follow the directions on the package *exactly*. And keep poisons out of the reach of children and pets. Malathion is a good general chemical that does not have an accumulative effect. If you use any chemical insecticide, always follow these five rules:

1. Never use a chemical on a bone dry plant.
2. Never spray plants in direct sun.
3. Use a spray at the proper distance as marked on the package.
4. Try to douse insects if they are in sight.
5. Do not use chemicals on ferns.

INSECTS AND DISEASES

Here are some chemical pesticides and their applications:

CHEMICAL	USED AGAINST	REMARKS
Malathion	Aphids, mites, scale	Broad-spectrum insecticide; fairly nontoxic to human beings and animals
Diazinon, Spectracide	Aphids, mites, scale	Good but more toxic than Malathion
Sevin	All kinds of insects	Available in powder or dust form
Isotox, Meta-Systox	Most insects	Systemics; toxic but effective
Black Leaf 40	Aphids and other sucking insects	Tobacco extract; relatively toxic but safe for plants
Pyrethrum, Rotenone	Aphids, flies, other household pests	Botanical insecticides; generally safe
Aerosol bombs	Most insects	Can harm leaves if sprayed too close, and can irritate your lungs (do not use an outdoor brand for indoor plants)

Diseases

Plant diseases rarely start in the window greenhouse if plants are healthy and robust. But botrytis, fungi, and other diseases may hit your plants and can cause trouble unless treated early. Disease symptoms include spots, rings, rot, and mildew. At these first signs isolate affected plants and use the remedies given below.

INSECTS AND DISEASES

Fungicides

Your main control over plant diseases is found in fungicides—chemicals that kill or inhibit the growth of bacteria and fungi. Fungicides come in several forms. Here is a resume of available fungicides:

CAPTAN—a generally safe fungicide, effective in controlling many diseases.
KARANTHANE—highly effective for many types of powdery mildew.
ZINEB—used for many bacterial and fungal diseases.
BENOMYL—makes plants resistant to bacterial and fungal infection.
SULFUR—an old but reliable fungicide that controls many diseases.

As with all chemicals, use them carefully as directed on the package. Keep all containers out of the reach of children and pets.

If you object to chemicals in the home, you can guard against diseases by reducing the humidity in the greenhouse and providing excellent ventilation. Avoid overfeeding, and always be sure plants and pots are scrupulously clean. These factors go a long way in keeping diseases from striking plants.

Window Greenhouse Suppliers

At present writing, the following listed suppliers offer prefabricated window greenhouses of various types. Write for catalogs and information. No doubt there will be more companies making window greenhouses as time goes by.

Aluminum Greenhouses Inc.
14615 Lorain Avenue
Cleveland, Ohio 44111

Grow House Corporation
2335 Burbank Drive
Dallas, Texas 73235

WINDOW GREENHOUSE SUPPLIERS

Lord and Burnham Inc.
Irvington, New York 10533

Feather Hill Industries Inc.
Box 41
Zenda, Wisconsin 53195

Rohm and Haas
Independence Mall
Philadelphia, Pennsylvania 19106

Index

acrylic, in construction, 28-30
Adiantum, 77-78
Aechmea, 73
African violets, 14, 56, 64, 67, 68, 103
ageratum, 82
Allium neopolitanum, 87
Allophytum mexicanum, 87
Althaea rosea, 82
aluminum, in construction, 28
alyssum, 83
'America' spinach, 95
Angraecum compactum, 71
annuals, 55, 56, 80-84, 96
anthuriums, 57, 87-88
Antirrhinum majus, 82
Aphelandra chamoissiana, 88
aphids, 104, 105, 108, 111
Artelisia dracunculus, 98
Asocentrum, 71
asters, 82, 85
Astilbe japonica, 85

'Baby Doll,' 68
'Baby Perfectifolia,' 69
'Baby Rainbow,' 69
baby's breath, 86
bachelor's button, 83
basil, 96
beets, 92
begonias, 12, 55, 56, 65, 69-70, 77, 103
'Bell Boy Hybrid,' 94
bellflower, 85
'Berry Autumn,' 70
'Big Boston,' 94
bird's-nest fern, 76, 78
'Black Beauty,' 93
black-eyed Susan, 89
'Black Falcon,' 70
blanketflower, 86
Blechnum brasiliense, 78
blood lily, 88
'Bonanza,' 68
bone meal, 59, 87

115

INDEX

Boston fern, 76
botrytis, 111
Bougainvillea, 88
'Bow Chance,' 70
'Bow Joe,' 70
bracing, 19, 21
bromeliads, 12, 55, 56, 64, 73-74
bulbous plants, 55, 57
'Burpee's Fordhook,' 94
'Butter Crunch,' 94

cacti, 59, 65-67
caladiums, 19, 64
calatheas, 57
Calendula officinalis, 82
Callistephus chinensis, 82
campanulas, 56, 86, 88
Capanemia uliginosa, 71
'Carita,' 68
carrots, 92-93
casement windows, 40
Cattleya walkeriana, 71
cedar heartwood, in construction, 25
Centaurea cyanus, 83
'Chantilly Lace,' 70
chemical insecticides, 109-111
  how to use, 110
  types of, 111
'China Doll,' 70
chrysanthemum, 85
cineraria, 83-84
Cobeae scandens, 83
Coelogyne orchracea, 71
coleus, 83
columneas, 56, 67, 68
compost, 59, 69, 87, 92
containers, 39, 69, 77, 81
  cleaning of, 62
  and disease, 112
  for starting seed, 101, 103
  for vegetables, 92
cornflower, 83
crassulas, 65, 66
cucumbers, 93
cuttings, 99, 102-103

Davallia fejeensis, 78
delphinium, 85-86
Dendrobium pierardii, 71
Dendrochilum filiforme, 72
'Detroit Dark Red,' 92
Dianthus, 83
dieffenbachias, 56, 59, 74, 80
dill, 96
diseases, 105, 111-112
double-hung windows, 3, 40
dracaenas, 56, 59, 79

east windows, *see* south and east windows
Echinocactus, 66
Echinocereus, 66
Echinopsis, 66
eggplant, 93
Epidendrum, 71
episcias, 56, 67, 68
Eucomis punctata, 88

false spirea, 85
'Fancy Doll,' 68
fans, 37
feeding, fertilizers, 60-61, 66, 67, 69, 74, 75, 76, 87, 92, 102
  and disease, 112
  rules for, 61
  in starting seed, 102
  time-release, 60
ferns, 56, 76-78, 110
ficuses, 57
fir bark, 71, 73
fish emulsion, 61, 66
flamingo flower, 87-88
flashing, 21
flossflower, 82
flowering onion, 87
flowering plants:
  for north windows, 19
  soil for, 59
  for south and east windows, 18, 55
  for west windows, 19, 56
'Fluffy Ruffles,' 78

116

foliage plants:
    for north windows, 19, 74
    for south and east windows, 18, 74
    for west windows, 19, 56, 74
fungicides, 112

Gaillardia aristata, 86
geraniums, 65
germination, 102
gesneriads, 56, 65, 67-68
ginger lily, 88
glass, in construction, 28-31
Gloxinia, 68
'Gold Pak,' 93
growing conditions, 17, 53-62
growing mediums, 101
Guzmania lingulata, 74
Gymnocalycium, 66
Gypsophilia paniculata, 86

Haemanthus coccineus, 88
hammers, 24
hardware cloth, 35, 54
haworthias, 65, 66
heating, *see* temperature
Hedychium coronarium, 88
herbs, 18, 56, 59, 96-98
hollyhock, 82
Hoya carnosa, 88
humidity, 17, 73, 79, 80, 103
    and disease, 112
    in starting seed, 101
humus, 69, 87
hydrangeas, 16, 64
Hypocyrta, 68

impatiens, 83
injection-molded window greenhouses, 31-33
insecticides, 108-111
    chemical, 109-111
    old-fashioned, 108-109
insects, 104-111
'Irish Elf,' 68

Jacobean lily, 89
'Japanese Hybrid,' 93
Jiffy Pellets, 101

Kalanchoe, 66-67
Kerfersteinia gramineus, 72
Kohleria amabilis, 68

Lantana montevidensis, 88-89
larkspur, 85-86
leaf cuttings, 103
leaf mold, 76
leaves, browning of, 60
ledger strips, 21
Leptotes bicolor, 72
lettuce, 91, 94
lice, plant, 105, 108
light exposure, 17
    in interior window greenhouses, 33-34
    in plant selection, 54-57, 66, 67, 69, 71, 73, 74, 75, 76, 79, 80, 86, 92, 96
    for starting seed and cuttings, 101, 103
'Little Finger,' 92-93
'Little Mo,' 68
loam, 75, 76, 79
Lobivia, 67
Lobularia maritima, 83
location of window greenhouses, 13-15, 17, 18-19
'Lucy Closson,' 70
lumber, in construction, 25
Lycaste aromatica, 72

Malathion, 110, 111
marantas, 57
marigolds, 82, 84
marjoram, 97
Masdevallia, 72
materials, construction, 25-31
mealybugs, 104, 105, 108
miniature plants, 63, 64-67
'Minikin,' 68

INDEX

mites, 104, 105-107, 111
moss pink, 86

nasturtium, 84
Neoregelia carolinae tricolor, 74
Nephrolepis, 78
Nidularium, 74
north windows, plant selection for, 19, 54, 56-57, 74, 76

'Oakleaf,' 94
Oncidium ampliatum, 72
orchids, 12, 16, 55, 56, 64, 65, 70-72
Oriental poppy, 86
Ornithocephalus bicornis, 72
oxalis, 56

palms, 57, 60
Papaver orientale, 86
parodias, 65, 67
parsley, 97
'Patio Pik' cucumbers, 93
'Patio Pik' tomatoes, 95
peacock plant, 56
peat cubes, 101
peat moss, 75, 79
peppers, 91, 94
perennials, 55, 56, 80, 85-86, 96
Petrea volubilis, 89
petunias, 81
philodendrons, 56, 74, 75-76
phlox, 83, 86
Phyllitis scolopendrium, 78
pineapple lily, 88
pink, 83
planter bins, metal, 38, 39, 81
plant food, *see* feeding, fertilizers
plant list, for beginners, 18-19
plastics, in construction, 28-30
Platycerium, 78
Platyclinis, 72
Polypodium polycarpon, 78
Polystichum, 78
pots, *see* containers
potting, 61-62, 79, 102

prefabricated window greenhouses, 4, 5-6, 8, 12-13, 31-33, 34
prestarted plants, 81, 92
Pteris ensiformis, 78

queen wreath, 89

rabbit's-foot fern, 76, 78
rebutias, 65, 67
Rechsteineria cardinalis, 68
'Red Berry,' 70
'Red Cherry,' 95
red spider mites, 104, 105-107
redwood, in construction, 6, 12, 25, 34
Rootone, 102
Rosa chinensis minima, 89
'Rosa Kugel,' 70
rosemary, 97
'Ruby Queen,' 92
Ruellia macrantha, 89

sage, 98
'Salad Bowl,' 94
sand, 59, 66, 75, 76, 79, 96
savory, 98
saws, 24
scale, 107, 108, 111
Schizocentron elegans, 89
screwdrivers, 24
Sedum, 67
seed, starting, 81, 91, 92, 99-102
Senecio cruentus, 83-84
Shasta daisy, 85
shelves and supports, 8, 12, 34-37
sinningias, 67, 68
sliding windows, 7, 40
snapdragon, 82
snow protection, 23
soil, 58-60, 66, 67, 69, 73, 74, 75, 76, 79, 80, 81, 87, 92, 96
soilless mixes, 59
south and east windows, plant selection for, 18, 54-55, 80, 86
Spanish shawl, 89

'Spaulding,' 70
spinach, 95
Sprekelia formosissima, 89
staghorn fern, 78
starting mediums, 81, 101, 102, 103
Stelis, 72
strap-leaf fern, 78
Streptocarpus, 68
succulents, 59, 65-67
sulfur, 112
'Summer Bibb,' 94
sweet william, 83
sword fern, 78

Tagetes erecta, 84
tarragon, 98
temperature, 17, 37, 73, 75, 80, 101
thermometers, 37
thrips, 107, 109
Thunbergia alata, 89
thyme, 98
'Tiny Dill Cuke,' 93
'Tiny Tim,' 95
tomatoes, 91, 95
tools, construction, 23-24
trays, *see* containers
Tropaeolum majus, 84

vegetables, 90-95
  soil for, 59, 92
  for south and east windows, 18, 55, 92
  for west windows, 18, 56
ventilation, 67
  construction for, 12, 16, 23, 29, 35
  and disease, 112

regulation of, 7, 37
  in starting seed, 101
vermiculite, 81, 101
'Verona,' 78
'Victoriae,' 78
Vriesia, 74

watering, 57-58, 65, 67, 71, 73, 74, 75, 77, 80, 81, 87, 90, 96, 101
wax plant, 88
west windows, plant selection for, 18-19, 54, 56, 76
window greenhouses:
  advantages of, 7-8, 10
  attachment of, 21, 25
  construction of, 20-52
  cost of, 5, 6, 8, 13
  growing conditions in, 17, 53-62
  heating of, 37
  homemade, 5-6, 7, 9, 11, 12-13, 20-52
  injection-molded, 31-33
  interior-type, 5-6, 33-34
  location of, 13-15, 17, 18-19
  materials for, 12-13
  outside-type, 5-6
  practical aspects of, 11-13
  prefabricated, 4, 5-6, 8, 12-13, 27, 29, 31-33, 34, 35, 39, 113-114
  selecting plants for, 15-17, 18-19
  size of, 4, 6
  suppliers of, 113-114
windows, types of, 3, 40
'Winter Bloomsdale,' 95

zinnia, 84